TRUSTY AND WELL BELOVED

William Harness in the uniform of the 65th Foot, *c.* 1787.

TRUSTY AND WELL BELOVED

THE LETTERS HOME OF WILLIAM HARNESS
AN OFFICER OF GEORGE III

Edited by

Caroline M. Duncan-Jones

LONDON

S·P·C·K

1957

First published in 1957
by S.P.C.K.
Holy Trinity Church
Marylebone Road
London N.W.1
Printed in Scotland by
Gilmour and Dean Ltd., Glasgow

14.253.

Acknowledgements

My THANKS are due to the Librarian of the India Office Library for the translations of the names of Indian servants and the identification of certain place names; to the Chief Library Clerk of the Royal United Service Institution for details about the army record of William Harness, for an account of the wreck of the transport *Arniston*, and for the pictures facing pp. 35 and 134; to the Director of the Egyptian Education Bureau for verifying names of places; to Captain J. M. Carew for permission to make quotations from Fortescue's *A History of the British Army*; and to the Editor of the *Cornhill* for permission to use some letters that appeared in an article in that magazine in February 1939.

Contents

Illustrations

Foreword

It is a fascinating occupation to dip into a collection of old family letters and from the faded ink and criss-cross writing to form a picture of the little daily doings and the bigger joys and sorrows of a bygone generation. My family has always been much given to the hoarding of correspondence. In looking through boxes which contain some hundreds of letters and records of my forebears, the Harnesses, a family of honourable, ordinary English stock, I have found there a mirror of a life which, less than two centuries ago, had a spaciousness and a fragrance, combined with hardships and limitations, of which we have little conception to-day. These letters, simple and common-place as they often are, have a savour, a dignity and a courtesy that are seldom found in our present hurried, telegraphic correspondence.

Among the silhouettes on my wall are the likeness of a military officer wearing a cocked hat, with a cockade, his hair tied back in a queue; and opposite him a pretty boy in a ruffled shirt, his long hair curling on to his shoulders. The soldier is my great-great-great-uncle, William Harness, an officer in the 80th Regiment of Foot. The boy is his son, Charles. It is their family history which is set forth by their letters in these pages.

The letters tell a story of adventurous service in foreign lands and of long periods of separation, coupled with glimpses of quiet, happy domestic life at home. The Harnesses were not rich or influential people; but they had their standards of " genteel " and cultivated living, to which they clung and to which they rightly attached a vast importance. Their standards are not, of course, the standards of to-day. It would not, for instance, have occurred to Elizabeth Harness to keep less than three maids; and this, even with her modest income, she was able to do. She was fully conscious of her dignity as a " major's lady " and, at the same time, a good neighbour and a considerate and kindly mistress. She and her William were a tenderly devoted couple and wise and loving parents. In the short years that they and their children were able to spend together they found life very good. Here then is their story as told by themselves.

C. M. D.-J.

1

A Long Engagement

YOUNG William Harness, when still a very junior officer in the army of His Majesty King George III, fell in love with Miss Elizabeth Bigg. This lady lived with her mother and her aunts —her father's sisters—at Aylesbury. Her father, described variously in the parish registers as Thomas Bigg, Gentleman, or Thomas Bigg, Attorney, had died in 1775, when his daughter, an only child apparently, was 10 years old. She had several relations living in and about Aylesbury, some of whom were farmers, and the family appears to have borne its part in political elections and in social events that took place in the little County Town. The first glimpse of Elizabeth Bigg appears in a letter written by one of the aunts to her niece when she was away at school. It tells of gay doings at Aylesbury and, incidentally, shows that the Biggs and the Harnesses were already acquainted. Miss Bigg writes:

It was my intention to have wrote to my dearest Betty the last time Mr Shirman came, but was prevented. I will now endeavour to collect all the News that is stirring to transmit to my Dear Child. Some of it is of the Melancholy Mind, of this sort is the death of Miss Betsey Harness. I am sincerely concerned for her. She was a good natured, obliging girl, and in my Eye one of the *Flowers* of Aylesbury.

Before proceeding any further I have the Pleasure to tell you that the Map arrived safe on Monday morning. Your Mama sent immediately for a Carpenter and had it hung up in one of the Niches in the best Parlour. I assure you my Dear Girl that we all set a very high Value upon it, and when you have finished Miss Stephens's Apron, to oblige me I hope you will work the Map of Europe. Your Mama will talk to your Governess about it when she comes to see you. Missey Smith

1

is to go to your School, I believe the latter end of next week. You will then have *another Child.* Your Aunt Croke goes to Oxford next Tuesday, We shall be very lonely without her.

You know the Races were this week; Monday was a delightful Day, and to speak in the Language of the Gentlemen of the Turf, there was exceeding good sport, but so little Company in Town that *Lady Say* was obliged to exert all her powers of Rhetoric to make up six Couple for a Dance at the George. Tuesday there was a fine Breakfast as usual, a Race in the Morning, another in the afternoon and a Ball in the Sessions Hall at night of fourteen Couple.

Captain Grenville has advertised to represent the County in the room of his Brother. Your Uncle Jerry and Mr Parker are at this time canvassing for him. An opposition is talked of, Mr Hampden is said to be the Gentleman intended. Most of the Gentry went out of Town on Wednesday Morning. I did not think the diversion of the Day worth an enquiry, my attention was differently engaged. Mr Grenville, attended by Sir John Vanhatten, Mr Jerry Bigg, Mr Fricker and another Gentleman, went to all the Freeholders to desire their Votes and Interest and to invite them to supper at the George. I have not yet heard who accepted the Invitation. In the Afternoon Mrs Vanderhelm and Miss, Miss Hawkins, Miss Constable, Miss Lydia and Miss Molly Bigg all drank Tea and spent the evening with us.

A fine and varied budget of news, sporting, social, and political, to amuse the small Elizabeth. Evidently this 7-year-old was a busy little girl, as little girls had to be in her day. The two samplers which decorated the niches in the best parlour—one a map of the counties of England and the other, as requested, of the countries of Europe—remain as products of her diligence, witnesses to many sedentary hours accompanied, perhaps, by occasional tears.

Elizabeth's father and mother, Thomas Bigg and Elizabeth Evans, were married at Aylesbury Parish Church in October 1764. The witnesses were Jeremiah Bigg—the Uncle Jerry of the letter—and another brother-in-law, Alexander Croke of Studley Priory in Oxfordshire. The grandmother of Elizabeth Evans, Mrs Sarah Stephens of Shrivenham in Berkshire, had

2

left a will which is full of entertaining detail and which brings to our notice some other members of the family.

To her unmarried daughter, Alethea, she left " all my wearing Apparel, all my Rings ", silver spoons, household linen, " all my Tea things as Teapots Cups Saucers Stands Spoons Tongs Silver Saucepan Tea table Tea board my Copper Coffeepot my Coffee Mill and Stand " and the use of all her mother's household goods so long as it was " convenient " for her to live in Shrivenham. Should she leave Shrivenham she was to have " the Furniture of my best Chamber that is the Parlour Chamber ". Another daughter received " my best broad Stript Ticking Featherbed a pair of Pillows a pair of Blankets a Quilt a broad Striped Bolster a Bedstead a Set of Blew Curtains Valens and Tester ". To her daughter, Margaret Evans, the mother of Elizabeth, she left " the furniture of the Hall Chamber ". Her two granddaughters, Elizabeth, the future Mrs Bigg, and Sarah Evans, who married Alexander Croke, received respectively " six Damask Napkins and my little Damask Tablecloath ". If Alethea Stephens should leave Shrivenham £5 was to be given to the poor. " I desire that every poor Widow in the Parish may have half a Crown if the Five pound will do it."

Alethea Stephens did leave Berkshire and we find her later living near Bath with her brother, Dr James Stephens, also apparently unmarried, a kindly, though slightly dictatorial, great-aunt and great-uncle to the younger Elizabeth. We have seen already that " Miss Stephens's Apron " was a task that could not be put on one side by a little girl who may perhaps have found the prospect of the map of Europe more enticing.

A cousin of the two Elizabeths was Mary Welch, who became the wife of the famous sculptor, Joseph Nollekens. The Nollekens were an eccentric, rather unpleasant couple, but they both remembered their young cousin, Elizabeth Harness—as she was by that time—in their wills. Mrs Nollekens was the daughter of that astonishing person, Saunders Welch, who, having been brought up in Aylesbury workhouse, was apprenticed to a trunk-maker at the corner of St Paul's Churchyard and became eventually High Constable of Westminster and one of His Majesty's Justices of the Peace for that city. He was the intimate friend of Dr Johnson, to whom he left five guineas, and who called him in a letter " one of my best and dearest friends ".

The Biggs were evidently a well established family at Aylesbury as is shown by frequent entries in the church registers; but it is not clear what brought William Harness to that county and to a commission in the Bucks Militia. The " good natured, obliging girl " who was a " Flower of Ayles- bury " must have been a relation, but his roots appear to have been in the West Country. A cousin, Samuel Harness, was Vicar of Stowford in Devon. William's brother, John, seven years his senior, was a distinguished naval surgeon, who proposed and carried out a successful treatment for scurvy. He was a friend of Lord Nelson, who was godfather to his daughter, and it is probable that he was one of the doctors called in after Nelson had lost his eye. He, and his son after him, were the friends and trustees of Mrs Mitford and her famous daughter, Mary Russell Mitford,[1] and were able, with some difficulty, to prevent Mary's disgraceful old father from squandering the last remnant of his hard-working daughter's money. Another friend of John Harness was Admiral Lord Collingwood, who at the Battle of Trafalgar, as is recorded on his memorial in Newcastle Cathedral, " led the British Squadrons into action and pressed forward with his single ship into the midst of the combined fleets of France and Spain. On that day after the death of his illustrious commander and friend Lord Nelson, he completed the most glorious and decisive victory that is recorded in the naval annals of the world ". Some four weeks after the battle this " pious just and exemplary man " wrote to Doctor Harness at the Sick and Hurt Board in Somerset Place.

Queen, Gib[r] bay, 19 November 1805

My dear Sir,

I am sure no one would more sincerely rejoice in our success than you would—it has been great indeed—and we have much reason to be thankful but alas! amidst our joy we have also great cause of lamentation in the death of our excellent friend Lord Nelson—who was killed by a musket ball—and many others we have had of highly estimable character—Duff and

[1] See my *Miss Mitford and Mr Harness: Records of a Friendship*, 1955. C.M.D.-J.

Cooke were my friends—and cannot remember their fall but with great grief. My ship shattered and torn is gone to England—and in her is Mr Lloyd the surgeon—a man for whose skill and character I have a great respect—and wish very much to be of service to him—I would be much obliged if you could remove him into some situation where he might not go to sea again. I intend to do him all the kindness I can for he deserves it—and would be glad if he could in the mean time be appointed to anything stationary that would prevent his going to sea again—I believe if it is in your power you will oblige me—I shall receive it as a very great kindness.

I hope your sons are well, and am my dear Sir with great regard

Your faithfull Humble Serv.,

Cutht. Collingwood

I am growing very feeble—and very old—worn to a thread.

William Harness was not content to remain an officer of the militia. He hoped to acquire a commission in the regular army. He was at Banbury when, in December 1799, he received from Lord Hampden a welcome letter which told of the possibility of his appointment to an " ensigncy in an old corps ". Three months later there came a note from the Commander-in-Chief of the forces in Great Britain.

Lord Amherst presents his Compliments to Lord Hampden, and has the honour to acquaint his Lordship that having recommended to The King Mr William Harness, of the Bucks Militia, to be an Ensign in the 65th Regiment of Foot,[1] His Majesty has been pleased to approve of him accordingly.

Whitehall, 10 February 1780

William had been for about four years an officer in the 65th Regiment when he realized that his love for Elizabeth Bigg was returned. He was then a hard-working soldier, a good, upright, and capable but sadly impecunious young man. From Dublin, where he was stationed, he wrote in rounded, decorous terms and long complicated sentences to declare his eager affection.

---

[1] Now the York and Lancaster Regiment.

5

5 December 1784

My dear Miss Bigg knows how to pardon, where the heart, overflowing with such sentiments as the most ardent love and the most unbounded gratitude inspire, breaking beyond the bounds of too obdurate duty, eagerly seeks to justify and to make know[n] its feelings. Conscious of each devious step, I am sensible of and apprehend the decision of deliberate reason; but forgive me if these sensations, with which my soul is at present occupy'd, will not be confined. No, lovely and too Generous Girl, in vain were the endeavour to withhold what my whole Soul is but too anxious to disclose. My Love, my admiration have long been and will be for *ever and* for *ever* Yours, but how or in what Language shall I describe what I feel in learning the effects of the tender sensibility you discovered on the melancholy event which robbed me of a dearly beloved, the Best, the kindest, the most indulgent, the most affectionate of Fathers. In you I have found the only source of consolation. You, my ever charming friend, have been my only and constant support. Nothing shall ever tear from my Memory the eternal obligations, the tender, the *delicious* sense of the purest gratitude I owe to your sollicitude, to your generosity and to your humanity.

Would to God the blissful moment would arrive when the World will testify my truth, and envy me my fate! In the mean while happy, *inexpressibly happy*, in the possession of *your esteem*, the study of each day shall be to *value* and to *merit* your approbation. One of the evils to which my singular destiny reduces me consists in the reflection that, however pure my affection, however sacred my intentions, the inviolable attachment I shall for ever cherish for my *dear*, my *dearest Eliza* should want the sanction of her much respected Mother. Her anxiety for your happiness is with me an additional motive of respect. I must admire and lament that uneasiness I fear I am doomed to cause, but which I would give worlds to remove.

In your felicity and welfare is placed my future peace. Be happy! and honour me with a stray or wandering thought. *Adieu thrice dear* and *beloved* girl!

I am, *for ever yours*

W. H.

Honor me—shall I entreat it?—honor me with a Line.

Evidently the course of youthful love did not at first run smoothly. There is further proof of this in a letter from the lady, written perhaps in response to William's touching postscript. She writes in an elegant, sloping hand and the ardour of her affection is masked indeed, but not hidden, under the stilted and dutiful propriety of her style. There is no address or date.

One of the best of men will, I flatter myself, excuse my entering on a correspondence with him clandestinely, but will with me think it inconsistent with the duty I owe to the most indulgent of Mothers. Let this one letter for the present suffice; some happier period may arrive when I may be allowed by my dearest friends the privilege of writing to you. Until then be content with only hearing of me through the kind friendship of your valuable correspondent, who I know from his native goodness of Heart will take pleasure in adding favours to the many we have already received from him. As I must be convinced that Interest has had no share in your attachment to me, I will therefore place the most implicit faith in the affection you profess. My sentiments in regard to yourself you are not a stranger to, but I cannot be happy whilst I feel a consciousness of doing wrong by engaging in an affair of the greatest consequence to myself and friends, without their knowledge and approbation. Yet I have much to hope from the good opinion my mother entertains of you, and I know she is not ignorant that you *once* had a partiality for me. I wish I could take courage and disclose the whole, but at present I find myself unequal to the task. How happy have I been made, when at any time your name has been mentioned, to hear my mother join in praising and speaking of you in the highest terms possible. In short she believes you to be a truly good young man, the principal requirement, I'm sure, she would wish for in the Husband for her child; and I am certain her views for me are not beyond a genteel sufficiency to support me in the station in which I have been bred up. Trusting in your constancy I will endeavour to be as happy as I can, and will with you repose the whole on the mercy of a just Providence and with patience wait the event.

Your Brother Richard often pleasures us with his company.

He is a sensible clever little fellow and a great favourite with us *all*—with everybody and not the less so with *me* for the great resemblance he bears to *a certain friend of mine* who is seldom absent from my thoughts. Good health and happiness constantly attend you is the sincere wish of her who will be

Ever yours

E. B.

Probably the lack of a " genteel sufficiency " was the only obstacle in the way of Mrs Bigg's approval of their engagement, but it was some seven years before that sufficiency was attained. During that long time of waiting they did not often meet. Once they were over two years separated, for William had to go where his profession took him and travelling was slow and expensive—not for him the delight of dashing off to spend week-ends with his lady's family. Before long, however, the ban on correspondence was lifted and William wrote long letters from Doncaster, Scarborough, Sheffield, Dover, Nottingham, London, and several other places, giving his Elizabeth accounts of his marches, his numerous social engagements, and of the different posts where his regiment was quartered. Always there was the undercurrent of longing for an improvement in his circumstances that would bring the long-drawn, wearisome engagement to an end. So irksome at one time did William find the trials of waiting and separation that, keen soldier though he was, he had in 1786 serious thoughts of changing his profession.

Sunday 23 September

I saw the other day the presentation of a living advertized, the annual income from a hundred and fifty to two hundred pounds a year; it is situated in Suffolk. Curiosity led me to inquire the terms and I find fourteen hundred pounds are required. There is no profession I would not try or sacrifize I would not make. I have written a second letter on the subject of the Rectory and will tell you more when I have an answer. Assured of your wishes for our union I have ventured, Betsy, to offer a thousand pounds for the Succession. I could hold a curacy with it, which would make an addition you know. Our income would consequently be greater than were we to succeed

8

to the Adjutancy it would be. It is expected to be vacant in a few days. Six months would be all that would be requisite for my attaining *Priest's* Orders. How strange does it sound.

Strange indeed! A commentary on the curious state of affairs which the Church in the eighteenth century was able, through its undying spiritual vitality, to surmount and survive. And we need not doubt that, had William Harness seen fit to take orders, he would have proved like many in his day and according to his lights, a true and faithful parish priest. That same evening he added some sentences to his letter.

I have this afternoon received a full account. The house is small, One Parlour, a Hall convertible at a small expense into another Parlour, four Bed Chambers, proportionate Stabling and Offices, a good neighbourhood at a short distance and no dirty Villages near or *Great Man in the Parish*, the whole clear of Church and poor Rates and Twelve Hundred Guineas the least that would be taken for the Presentation.

Mr Harness did not feel himself " justified in finding so large a sum " and the dream of the parish and house " in every way sufficient for the comfort of our lives " faded away.

When William Harness first became engaged to Elizabeth he was still an ensign in the 65th Regiment of Foot. A few years later he changed to the 29th (now the Worcestershire Regiment). Lord Henry Fitzgerald, " an excellent young man " with " elegant manners " and " very affable ", was Lieutenant-Colonel in the 29th, and Lord Harrington, young Mr Harness's very kind friend and patron, was in 1788 appointed to the command of this, his old regiment. At the age of 35 he already had several years of distinguished service behind him. It was he who was responsible for William's transfer to his own regiment.

For the best part of two years William Harness was stationed at Nottingham, which he found " outrageously gay; Assemblies and Balls eternally."

While I boast of Oeconomising, my weekly expenditure exceeds two Guineas, and what is extraordinary it is out of my power to sink it a sixpence. We have a grand Concert here on Thursday and I am engaged to dance with Lady Caroline M'Kenzie.[1] Lady Caroline is Lord H's Niece, she is just of age, extremely beautiful and has fifty thousand pounds.

This was not the only occasion on which William was Lady Caroline's favoured partner. Indeed his servant, Thomas, went so far as to suggest that the lady would be an excellent match for his master; but even if William had not been far too sensible of Lady Caroline's exalted rank to contemplate such a possibility, his affections were too firmly rooted elsewhere. Elizabeth had no cause for anxiety.

A very happy feature of Mr Harness's stay in Nottingham was his intercourse with Lord and Lady Harrington and the frequent visits he paid to their home at Elvaston Castle, near Derby, where he was always a welcome guest. The following invitation is typical of many that William received from these good friends.

My dear Harness,

Should you be prevented from coming to Elvaston before Tuesday next, Lady Harrington and I hope that you will not fail to dine with us that day as we propose having our Turtle dressed on it. Col. Harneck desires his com^{ts} to you, and has now gott the Gray Poney by constant Exercise into such wind that He is ready to start Him against yours whenever you shall meet.

Believe me with much esteem
Your very faithful Friend and servant
Harrington

I hope you have not forgot our Cheeres and that you will make us as long a Visit as you conveniently can.

" Every hour I pass with him," wrote William once, " I fancy I leave him the better man."

Nottingham was not all concerts and assemblies. In 1787 William Harness found himself involved in a strenuous recruit-

[1] Daughter of the 5th Earl of Seaforth, who raised the Seaforth Highlanders. Her mother, who was Lord Harrington's sister, had died of consumption at the age of 19.

ing campaign. The air was full of rumours of war, and this was reflected in many of his letters.

There is nothing to apprehend from the War. The whole will, I doubt not, be terminated in a few months; the augmentation in the Army and the Marines the troubled state of Europe renders requisite. Nothing can be done before the Spring, and before that time either the Prussians will have left Holland or terms will be accepted. Promotion and a rapidity in the Recruiting Service are in my idea all the effects the Army will experience in the War.

I hoped when I began this letter to make it a long one. Yesterday was every hour of it taken up with Recruits and making returns. I had scarcely time to eat my dinner. This morning I rose early to give to my tenderly dear Bessy an hour, but before I got down stairs the house was full of people waiting for me. You can have no idea of the fatigue I have with Apprentices, Militia Men and a thousand imposing Villains, who are instantly carping at me. I am obliged to be civil to the vagabonds, whose whole design is to cheat me. I am now so well known (and the Party are in so high fame in the neighbourhood) and the additional Bounty that is now given are so many causes of confinement to me that I cannot even venture a walk in the Park without stealing it from the Service that has, for the last few days, entirely occupied me. With all this fuss I have only eight men attested in that time. My business is to discover frauds and to settle between masters for apprentices. I had not believed it possible there was so much fatigue attached to the idle (as it is esteemed) profession of a Recruiting Officer.

After an unfortunate experience in his first lodgings William found himself very comfortably settled at Nottingham. With him, always a stand-by and a comfort, was his faithful Thomas.

9 August 1787

I told you how I had been devoured by fleas and every sort of vermin. A second night was quite as much as I could stand and I returned on the next day to the Inn, where I remained till I heard of my present Lodgings, almost out of the Town in a retired part of it, with an old widow woman and her maid.

She is the picture of contentment and is cleanliness itself. I have a snug little parlour and comfortable rooms up stairs. The old lady bakes my bread and has procured Malt to brew for me, which she perfectly understands and will superintend Thomas in. She says too she can pickle and will give me all the assistance I wish of her. I foresee that we shall be very well together. She has offer'd to hang a gammon or two of Bacon in her chimney, cured after her own manner, and assures me it will be very good with a barn door chicken that will *now be coming in*, for little or nothing, after the harvest. I could not have got into a better house to oeconomise in. I pay her eight shillings a week for my rooms and furnish fire for the whole house.

Mr Harness's transfer to the 29th Regiment took him for a while to the West of England. The King was going to Cheltenham to drink the waters—a welcome emergence from the usual dull routine of his life. The courage and the homely virtues of " Farmer George " were at last becoming appreciated and gaining him some popularity. An affable letter from Lord Harrington gave our young officer his directions.

London, 9 July 1788

My dear Harness,

The 29th Regiment which was under orders to march for Derby (where it was to have remained till Scarbro' Castle was ready for its reception) is now by an express which is gone from the War office this Evening ordered to Glocester in order to do duty on the King during His residence at Cheltenham. We have so few officers with the Regiment that I wish very much you could contrive to join it as soon as possible at Gloucester for which place L^{dy} Harrington and I sett off on Friday morning. I shall be obliged to call in every officer whom I can get at. I hope to see you so soon that I will not take up your time farther than to assure you, of the sincere regard with which

I am ever,
My dear Harness,
your most affectionate Friend
and faithful Servant
Harrington

12

William set off without delay and from Tewkesbury, where he found the regiment, he wrote of the royal visit.

16 July 1788

I arrived at Cheltenham at one o'Clock yesterday. Their Majestys had been there since Saturday. They rode by just as I got into the Town. His Majesty rode first attended by Lord Courtoun, four footmen followed. The Queen and the Princess Royal in a Coach, one footman, the other two Princesses in another Coach and three footmen. Their Majestys have been here this Morning in the order in which I saw them at Cheltenham with the addition of two of his Equerries. The Town is now illuminated and my ears are stunned with the noise of bells, Guns and the rabble. They visited the Church and a Spa much of the nature of that of Cheltenham, which is about a mile distant from this Town. They go to the Worcester meeting which is hastened on their account.

Tewkesbury, 5 August 1788

We have so many Royal visits that the King passes thro' almost with so little Notice as the meanest of his Subjects. Cheltenham continues full of the best Companies. I have not been there since I past thro' it in my route hither. I think I mentioned the House the Royal Family reside in is so small as not to furnish a dressing Room for his Majesty. Two of the Princesses sleep in one small chamber. The Duke of York arrived at nine o'Clock of Friday Morning, having travelled all night. The King had breakfasted and immediately took him out to show him the most beautiful Country he had ever seen. They rode four hours and walked on the walks till dinner, at which His Majesty suffers himself to sit but ten minutes after the dinner is removed, His abstinence is wonderful. He says the only way to prevent eating much is to look for a great while at what you eat. After dinner they went to the play, the House was lighted with wax, a rich canopy hung over the Royal Box. They were received with plaudits which continued a quarter of an hour. The next morning they visited the Bishop of Worcester at the distance of forty miles and returned to dinner, after which his Royal Highness set off for London. It is wonderful the exercise they take.

At the "Worcester meeting" Mr Harness passed five gay days. The whole city was *en fête*.

Worcester is a beautiful city. A great deal of paint has been expended on it for the present occasion. The Company was very numerous, three thousand people were said to be present at the Messiah. The balls were much too crowded to admit of dancing with any satisfaction. Dr Chambers would have introduced me to Miss Greaves but she was engaged. I had promised myself a delightful conversation with my Bessy's friend, herself the subject. I find Miss G. is looked upon as a little capricious. I was at two assemblies; at one I danced with Miss Newport, a young lady of Worcester of Brome's acquaintance and at the other with Mrs Evans of Nottingham. I supped with them at the Dean's, who gave a supper to four hundred people. I had a thousand Compts from Nottingham friends. The Royal Family were at the Assembly the last night and an old friend of yours, Count Diss, who led Mrs Wells, the player, drunk into the room. Had my Bessy been there little would have been wanting to have made the five days I passed in Worcester perfectly happy.

On Saturday there was a public breakfast and dance at a bowling green, fitted up in great taste for the occasion. The different Companies of Traders made a grand display in processions with flags representing their several callings. His Majesty attended them one day to their Guild hall and drank a glass of wine to their prosperity. He visited the Porcelain manufactory, which is brought to great delicacy and perfection. The King paid a visit to Lord Harrington at the Inn and was surprized to find them at breakfast and still more to see Eggs on the table.

Malvern too had provided some quiet gaiety. "Malvern is most fantastically delightful," wrote William from Chesterfield on 10 September,

the Company all live at one house. Governor[1] and Mrs Hastings were there. After dinner Captain Nutt came to Brome and I with a petition from the Ladies that we would stay all night

[1] Warren Hastings.

and take a Dance in the Evening. There is a subscription
Harpsicord in the Long Room, the Ladies played by turns
accompanyed by a flute. I danced with the Miss Cartwrights
and a Miss Dolben, daughter to Sir William. Brome is returned
thither. I fear he is smitten.

The end of this year, 1788, was saddened by the death, at
the age of 20, of William's much loved young brother, Richard,
" that dear boy " as William often calls him. He was a pathetic
young man, who suffered much from bad health and was
apparently more than half in love with his sister-in-law-to-be.
He wrote frequently to Elizabeth, who behaved as the kindest
of sisters to him. After their father's death William Harness
and his elder brother had been greatly concerned with their
responsibility for the boy's future. It was planned to apprentice
him to Dr Midford [1] at Alresford.

20 March 1786
Mr Midford had agreed to take Richard without a premium,
but Mr B.[2] objected to his age as he would be three and
twenty by the expiration of his apprenticeship. They thought
too the many genteel acquaintances he has in Alresford would
be an obstacle in submitting to the Drudgery of their Shop.
You see, my dear, how strangely we have been abused. I
propose to offer Mr M. a Premium with him for five years
and should he not consent, tho' I have reason to think this will
do away many of his objections, I will write to the Druggist
who used to supply the Shop to look out for us.

This letter was written two years before Richard's death. He
was apprenticed eventually to an apothecary at Oxford.

For several months William's regiment was in barracks by
Scarborough Castle. He enjoyed Scarborough, where he had
a " very comfortable " room. In a letter of 1 October 1788 he
wrote:

I have given Thomas my Barrack furniture and have hired
a neat Bureau, Bed, a Glass, Mahogany Chairs, a Sopha and

---

[1] Later the doctor changed the spelling of his name to Mitford.

[2] Possibly Mr Blandy, Dr Midford's solicitor. The firm still exists in Reading.

a handsome table. I have purchased a Carpet, which is easy of carriage, and a window curtain which, with my boasted oeconomy, is to be converted into a Robe de Chambre. The Paper of the Room has a blue ground with large trees branching fantastically up it and intermixing their branches. The doors &c are painted white. I flatter myself I am rather smart.

There was a special reason for this grandeur, for he added that " Lady H. promised me she would drink some tea here when she arrives or probably I had been content with a simpler apartment ". As at Nottingham, so at Scarborough, Mr Harness found himself involved in a lively social round.

Lord Lincoln called on me the day after our arrival. I dined with him on Saturday. Lady Lincoln [1] told me she should have a few friends with her on the next evening and asked me to join them. Lady Ely and her mother, Mr and Mrs E. Lascelles, Lord Harrowby and his son Mr Ryder, two young Lascelles and Col. and Mrs Strickland were of the party. Mr Lascelles called on me yesterday and left a card from Mrs L. desiring my company to Tea in the Evening. Col. Strickland asked me to meet the same Company with Mrs Strickland this Evening. We had a very elegant Supper with Wist and Commerce. Nothing can exceed the civilities of Lord and Lady Lincoln. I was at the Rooms with them on Friday. Lady Lincoln congratulated me on my exchange. She knew her brother's *anxiety about it* and that it must be *particularly pleasing to him*. She asked me to her table at Commerce, introduced me to Lady Aberdeen and placed me between them.

An unpleasant feature of the time at Scarborough was duty in the guardroom.

Scarborough Castle, 16 March

This is a dismal night! I am on guard. A more wretched place than the Officers' Guardroom perhaps you never entered. This Guard is a new established thing. Major Campbell who, I believe, has a sincere desire of executing the wishes of Lord Harrington, in some instances dreadfully mistakes them. Out of sixty men (all we have capable of duty)

[1] Lord Harrington's sister.

five sentries are constantly, day and night, set to weather the constant tempests we are exposed to on this bleak point of land. The Scarbro' Guide will shew you its elevation. The violence of the wind I don't know how to describe to *you* who have always lived inland: I shall only say the heaviest men are often obliged to go on their hands and knees over the Draw-bridge, unable to stand against such violent gales. Our Guard-room was originally a Brew House, in its more prosperous days, but, with not uncommon fate of old age that oftener endures contempt than the veneration due to former worth, this worn-out Brew House was converted into a Hen Roost, and never to be sure was a poor decayed building so miserably used by its unworthy possessors. In addition to themselves they allow as fellow-lodgers toads spiders and creeping things innumer-able, but the Major looked with an eye of mercy on its horrors, and in his *humanity* ordered an officer in succession constantly to inhabit it. It once, as we may trace by the miserable remains, had a brick floor like better brew houses, and although its roof could boast no other covering than uncemented tyles there was a time when they were whole and impervious to the ruder elements; neither snow nor rain nor wind had then an entrance save at the door which was ever too small to fill the space between its crazy portals.

The parade of an Officer's Guard is enough to bring a host of *natives* every day at its mounting. My first was last Monday. I gave a breakfast to some ladies and all the officers, quite a pretty breakfast with a side table with cold ham and fowl &c &c, and after it a little concert till one, when this formidable business begins.

In May 1789 the regiment completed a march of a hundred miles from Scarborough through Whitby, Guisborough, Stockton, and Durham to Tynemouth. Stockton, " a very beautiful town in the Bishoprick, has a neat little Theatre and the Audience the evening we visited it was for a Country one unusually splendid ". For Durham William had no good word.

Tynemouth Barracks, 27 May 1789

Durham is a peninsula surrounded almost by the river Weire; it is the worst built Town in England, which it owes to its ecclesiastical Government. There are thirteen Prebends, the Dean and Chapter and Bishop, who by turns do duty in the Cathedral (a horrid Building where every order is set at defiance). The Resident constantly keeps an open table in a style truly princely, is served almost entirely out of gold. The Bishop is a little pontif and Durham, as far as the signs of Church discipline can be felt, a little Rome. The strongest execrations against the Clergy throughout the whole Bishoprick testify too how much the interests of religion are sacrificed to secular views.

Another Cathedral, which our soldier had visited, he had liked better.

Scarborough, 1 October 1788

York is a very old and irregularly built city, but quite the London of the little Gentry of the North. Its society is of course of the better kind, and from its cheapness must be a very desirable abode for people of small fortune. Its Cathedral is the most beautiful thing of the kind in England.

Having arrived at last at Tynemouth the regiment was received by the mayor.

27 May 1789

The People make a point of using every hospitality towards the Army. The Mayor came on Friday and gave us a public breakfast in a very elegant Barge quite " en gala ", an annual thing. He is quite the honest old English Hoste, full of good intentions. I do not know whether modern breeding does not set a greater value on the polish than the diamond itself. I do not say we are right, but sure there is much to reform in the bluntness of these advocates for honesty. One trait will give this man's character as well as a thousand. He cut in at Whist and got Lady Liddel for his partner, when shrugging his shoulders he crys out, " Ah! there it is now; if there is a fool in the Company I am sure to get her for a partner ". This exclamation, uttered in a tone that none but a Northumbrian can bear without pain, and addressed to a very elegant woman, gives so complete a picture of English independence, of English liberty and English wealth that I declare (I hope not as the Enemy of my Country) I could almost wish to see each of these national advantages we enjoy from our commerce and our laws so far restricted as would be necessary to enable us to pass through the world without insult from these well meaning good sort of people.

Having voiced the indignation aroused by the want of manners on the part of the mayor, William went on to comment on Elizabeth's own concerns. She was preparing for a long visit to Dr and Miss Stephens, now living at Camerton House near Bath, and her future husband—tactfully and carefully, for his Bessy had no shortcomings—welcomed the opportunity of her introduction to a wider society than that quiet circle to which she was accustomed.

In the autumn my beloved Girl goes to Camerton. I am happy at the opportunity given her of passing a few Months in a society that must both please and, perhaps I may say, instruct. I mean living so much in retirement you cannot see the changes that insensibly take place so readily as by mixing now and then with a better society than Aylesbury can afford you.

At Tynemouth there were " high debates on the subject of the Mess ". Mr Harness appears to have taken the lead among the junior officers and asked the major " whether we might not be able to make some reform in our manner of living, that our present expenses were infinitely beyond those of any other Regiment in the Service, that the consequences had been very severely felt by many of those Gentlemen who had lately been forced from their profession ". After much difficulty and opposition he was able to make better arrangements.

A confectioner, who has elegant rooms, has agreed to give us a good dinner every day for half a Guinea per head inclusive of wines. It is doing much to have knocked on the head that abominable practice of drinking.

Presumably the charge to the young officers was half a guinea weekly, not daily.

In October 1789 the regiment was preparing for a march of four hundred miles to Dover and William's mind was filled with anxious, eager planning for a meeting with Elizabeth on the route.

My adored Bessy, can you defer for one month your visit [to Bath]? I know not what plan to form, but could we not meet in Town on your way into Somersetshire? Lord H. expects the King will see us on the march so that I cannot ask leave to quit the Regiment, or I would leave it for a few days. I could stay the day after the Review in London. Devise some apology to Miss Stephens for putting off your visit. My Servant could attend you to Bath from London if your mama approves. His steadiness and sobriety have long been proved.

It was not only distance that made meetings hard to arrange. There were the claims of propriety to be considered. In the following February William was spending a long period of leave with his brother John's family at Wickham in Hampshire. William's brother and sister-in-law " express warm wishes " to make the acquaintance of Bessy, but such was the tyranny of social standards that she was not allowed to accept their invitation to stay.

Wickham, 7 February 1790

They are much concerned the hard opinion of the world must be bowed to. My brother calls by I know not what names the punctilio that robs us of the best of our enjoyments. My Bessy sees the force with which they bind. I with the deepest regret saw the difficulties.

It is hard to see exactly where the line was drawn between what was and what was not permissible, for the letter continues:

I think I have prevailed upon my Sister to endeavor to meet you next Summer in Buckinghamshire so that it may be permitted to her to be indulged with your Company here, She is an excellent little woman and independant of the esteem I should bear her as my brother's wife I feel for her the most lively friendship and regard.

He goes on to tell of his manner of life while staying at Wickham.

My Bessy is so good as to ask what I do? a question I find great difficulty to answer, not from the multiplicity of my occupations but from the indolence in which my time passes. Can I tell you I do nothing? which would be nearer the truth than any answer I could give. I have been twice to Portsmouth, once to Wotton and I think every other morning has been taken up with calling on people here or in the neighbourhood. Last evening has been the only one we have been alone. From this I would not have you infer my Sister keeps much Company, but here are just idle people enough to call in and saunter away the day with; but they are pleasant people. I have nothing to regret but the loss of my time.

Lord Albemarle [1] has called here three times since my being here and has presented my brother with a *very elegant* gold watch chain. His Lordship some time ago got a hurt in his Leg. My brother told the Surgeon what to do to it and the Leg soon recovered, and this is the method his Lordship has taken to shew my B. he was pleased with what he wrote.

On another occasion William determined to throw propriety to the winds. Elizabeth was staying in Welbeck Street and her mother's sister was living in Chancery Lane. " Monday Morning " is the only date on the letter.

I have determined at all event to be in Town on Thursday. The Diligence will arrive about seven in the Evening. Could I not that Evening see my adored Girl for an hour? Would it be amiss to go at once to Chancery Lane, where I could meet you as I come from the Coach and spend one blissful hour with my tenderly dear Girl? I then could come to you as I travel without the trouble of changing my Cloaths, which my Bessy would excuse. The Coach stops at the White Bear Piccadilly. Do, my dear, contrive to leave me a short note to the charge of the Bar, to be given to me on my arrival, telling me whether you approve my plan. I declare I can foresee nothing against it, and the perfect confidence the experience

---

[1] The 4th Earl of Albemarle succeeded his father, when an infant, in 1772, and so was 18 years old at the time of this letter.

of years has given you in your faithful H. will, I trust, do away every unnecessary objection to it on your part. The short time we have to pass together surely will not afford one Evening to be given to foolish forms. Then away with every barrier prudence itself declares useless.

Elizabeth made him some shirts and William was delighted at their comfort and " beautiful workmanship ". " I shall preserve ", he says, " with the choicest care your present. Nothing can fit better." In his directions for their making he had stipulated that the ruffles should not be of " an immoderate depth ", but added that " Kamsgatka does not furnish a man more ignorant in these matters than myself ". He sent Elizabeth a present of a toothpick case—a charming trifle of ivory bound with gold that is still in existence—and in an oval space in the cover set a miniature of himself; but, as he rightly says, " such a daub you never saw ".

William welcomed the news that Elizabeth was taking up " botanical studies ". " It is, I am told, a delightful science "; and he recommended " a very pretty Book come out lately by Dr Darwin [1] who translated Linnæus ". It is possible that Elizabeth's studies in botany consisted largely in flower painting, that attractive accomplishment in which the young ladies of the day often attained considerable skill; for in another letter William speaks of botany " being one of the prettiest amusements in the world " and hopes " to be presented by and bye with one of your drawings ".

Elizabeth had asked his advice about her reading. She had tried to organize a Book Club in Aylesbury, but had met with little success.

I wish to God I was able to direct your choice. Unfortunately the Books that might afford you the greatest pleasure and advantage are possibly most difficult to procure, but as a General Rule I shall *take the liberty* to say those that were written in the ages of Augustus, of Queen Elizabeth and Louis Quatorze are the Books that afford most amusement and are reckoned to be read with the greatest advantage. Many of

[1] Erasmus Darwin, the well-known physician and botanist, grandfather of Charles Darwin.

the last and present ages I think we should not be ignorant in, as the style is more suited to the conversation and letters of the present day.

His own reading, says William,

has been lately very confined. Mrs Piozzi's Book [1] and Moore's Letters are almost the whole I have read for some time, except a new Military publication. I am entering upon Frederick the Second of Prussia, a long work, or rather all his works collected in sixteen octavos in french; quite a work for the winter.

At Dover William Harness found himself in the midst of the trade which he calls " counterband ". It is an interesting sidelight on the standards and practices of the day that an upright, honourable young man could apparently take advantage of such trading without the slightest twinge of conscience.

12 December 1789

I have smuggled a good deal since I came to Dover. Every thing the East furnished or France produces there are shops in Dover which will furnish you—with a few execrations against Mr Pitt who, they say, is the greatest enemy their Trade ever felt. Should I be rich on leaving our quarters I mean to take the advantage of our baggage Waggons to conduct for me in safety a Cargo of Cambric, French Lace, China, Tea &c &c, a stock in provision. I am affraid Lady H. will spoil the market by going every day into every shop in search of whatever is valuable.

All things come to an end, even a long engagement; and in 1790 the " genteel sufficiency " that would allow of marriage was becoming a possibility. Already in March of that year Lord Harrington in one of his kindly notes had spoken of his wife's interest in the matter. " Lady Harrington begs her best compliments to you and hopes to hear e'er long that you are bound and fettered and in all things fitted by Hymen for the part of Benedict."

In the summer William began his preparations.

---

[1] Formerly Mrs Thrale, Dr Johnson's friend. The book was probably her *Anecdotes of the late Samuel Johnson, during the last twenty years of his life.*

2

Bride and Bridegroom

IN AUGUST 1790 the prospective bridegroom began to make ready a home for himself and his Elizabeth. As the engagement had been long, so the preparations for marriage were leisurely. In what was then the quiet village of Dronfield, near Chesterfield, William had discovered, probably during the long sojourn at Sheffield with the regiment, the little house that he desired. By 21 August, with the help of his " trusty Thomas " and a young fellow-officer named Brooke, he was already settling into the cottage, as he calls it. It seems a little hard to our twentieth-century feelings that Elizabeth herself should have had no share in getting ready the home of which William sent her such a satisfied description.

My beloved Bessy would have heard from me immediately had I not had my time wholly engaged in taking and fitting up a small house in this *salubrious* village. The smoke of Sheffield we found so very disagreeable that we sought for the readiest opportunity of quitting a place where it was not only mingled with the air we breathed, but made a principal portion of all we ate, drank or wore. Thomas you know is our Butler and factotum and a clever woman, whose youth was spent in service, cleans our house and does the washing.

Our garden we fortunately found tolerably supplied; our business for the two days we have been here has been to clear the paths. I in this Cottage should be the happiest of beings could you eat of the fruits of our Orchard, or repose yourself on the Seat we have made under the old tree that shelters our walk. We have expended fifty pounds in the furniture we immediately cannot do without.

Dronfield, 8 September 1790

Your Mama thinks our Cottage cheap. It is extremely so. All the taxes and rates on it of every kind I am told amount but to nine and twenty shillings annually. We have a seat in the Church and, what is of no use to us, unlimited right of Common. The Garden is not large, about five and sixty feet to each side the square. The Orchard has twenty-two fruit trees in it and about fifty or sixty Gooseberry and Currant trees. The Offices are much more than we can use and are very good. Our sitting room, which is of the best, is nearly fifteen feet square; the chamber out of it of the same size. The other front room is not quite so large but a tolerable room. The Kitchen is a very good one; the forth room is not a sitting room as the staircase comes into it and it opens into the yard. We have three Chambers as good as the rooms below and a fourth where Thomas sleeps, besides the Garrets. Pantrys and cupboards are innumerable and an excellent little archd Cellar (with sixty Gallons of ale by the bye). We found grates in all the rooms and a good dresser in the Kitchen. My Bessy you see how particular I have been.

The next letter furnished another example of the way in which scrupulously honourable people were prepared, apparently with no qualms, to defraud the government, or—looked at from another point of view—of the inevitable lawlessness produced by an iniquitous tax.

Dronfield, 24 September 1790

Captain Adams has a sale of the 4 & 6th of next month of very good furniture. I propose to purchase a few of the more necessary articles *we* may want, if it can be done with advantage. I think except one bed complete and *plate* and linen it would be advisable to sell all yours; perhaps a carpet or two may be spared. We have here two beds and a Servant's; one more and a Servant's would fill the Cottage and would be all we should require. I believe the additional window tax must have been left out of Mr Taylor's calculation. We have not yet paid any of any kind, but can say with confidence the taxes and rates will not amount to two Guineas annually. We have sixteen windows, but only pay for ten altho they are all open. It is the custom here for the person who inspects the windows to send round to desire the windows may be stopt, for that he shall come round on such a day, when every body have frames with paper in them and place them against the windows for the day. I was struck with surprize at a man coming to deliver his message at this house, when Thomas found in a Garrett six frames ready made for our purpose.

I take provisions to be nearly at the same price as what they are with you. Veal is four pence the pound and other meats at a half penny more. I have just given a poor woman four shillings for eight chickens. We had a Cart of coals drawn by three Horses, for which we paid four shillings brought into the yard. There are two pits within two miles.

Their income, he said, would be " very confined ", but

although we cannot expect to see much company, by all we shall be respected and by those we do see, I hope, esteemed. Our house will have in it nothing vulgar, nothing superfluous but everything useful, neat and necessary. Mr Taylor has a french man in his house, an Usher. We will engage him to improve our french, and with books, your work and my brush we shall be able to awaite what ever fortune give us with comfort and with pleasure.

Evidently William, like others of his family, had some talent for painting, enough at any rate to give him pleasure—Lady Harrington had once given him " a very elegant box of colours "; and we have seen that Elizabeth from an early age was clever with her needle. It is a happy scene that he conjures up with evenings of reading, drawing, skilled needlework, and some study of French. The two pits so conveniently near contained, however, a sad threat to the beauty of the countryside; and Dronfield is no longer the peaceful, " salubrious " village in which this young couple were so joyfully planning to make their home.

Elizabeth's letters of this time have not survived, so we have not her views on their future house; but we can see something of her feelings reflected in a letter of William's. " I long most earnestly to see you to talk over our plans and to hear you say you can retire into an almost wilderness with the man whose sole happiness is drawn from the love you bear him."

In addition to the preparation of the cottage there was another task to be fulfilled before the marriage could take place; indeed it was this undertaking that made marriage possible. At Lord Harrington's suggestion William Harness was appointed to raise an " independent company " [1] which would bring him a captaincy. " Sir Thomas Dundas," he wrote in November, " has written to his Agent in Ireland to raise me thirty or forty Irish recruits, so that I have every reason to believe I shall soon be complete and without costing me any money."

Of his recruiting experiences at Sheffield he wrote with gusto and evident enjoyment.

1 November 1790

I purposed to make Nottingham my head Quarters but, meeting with so great success here, I have sent Thomas there with a party and Major St Clair is good enough to look at my Recruits. I am exceedingly fortunate in my Subalterns. My Bessy wishes to know how to direct. All my letters from the War Office style me Captain and the King in my beating orders directs them to " Our trusty and well beloved William Harness Esqr Captain of Independent Company to be forthwith raised "; but I think it will be more modest in ourselves to preserve the Lieu^t till I am Gazetted, which I hope and trust will be very early in the Spring, if not earlier.

I wish you could see us march round; three or four Officers have been kind enough to go with me. Then follows a Cart with a Barrel of ale with fidlers and a Man with a Surloin of Roast Beef upon a pitch fork, then my Colours of yellow silk with a blue shield with a reath of oak leaves and trophies, and

[1] A company raised by an individual and afterwards drafted into corps that were short of their complement of men. Letters of service were issued from the War Office for the purpose of enabling " professional gentlemen " to attain rank, and also to recruit the army. It was a thoroughly bad system, open to many objections—expensive because, as soon as the men had been drafted out, half-pay had to be provided for their officers, and unfair because older men were passed over by boys who had been able to raise recruits cheaply. The system was discontinued when the Duke of York was appointed Commander-in-Chief. William Harness's company was disbanded in 1791.

in Silver letters on one side " Capt. Harness's Rangers ", on the other " Capt. Harness's Saucy Sheffielders ". My Sergeants, Corps, Drums and pipes and a string of Recruits close our line of march. You can conceive the stir in a prosperous place like this all this noise must make. I am become very popular.

William had hoped to meet Bessy during the march from Sheffield to Chatham, but at the bidding of Sir Thomas Dundas he altered his route.

25 November 1790

He pointed out the great risk of going near London with my Recruits, where there are so many Crimps [1] to delude them away, and offered to my consideration [a route] he had drawn out by Huntingdon and Essex to Tilbury fort.

By 17 December the newly formed company had passed through Cambridge and Saffron Walden and halted at Chelmsford.

I am now very busy fitting the Cloathing of my Company and cutting their Hair like Soldiers as I am anxious to march into Chatham in nothing inferior to our numerous Competitors for military fame.

It was not until 27 December that the company arrived at Chatham.

I was detained a week in Gravesend and only arrived here yesterday. The confusion I have had in arranging my company and in their examinations are more than I can name. My present strength is 91, very formidable. I am much flattered with this company, it is nearly the strongest which has marched into Chatham.

Some weeks later, we hear the last of the excellent servant, Thomas. He had recently married, which probably accounts for his desire for a more settled life.

[1] " An agent making it his business to procure seamen, soldiers etc., *esp.* by . . . decoying . . . or impressing them." (*Oxford English Dictionary*.)

Chatham, 2 February 1791

My faithful Thomas prefers being a Grocer at Nottingham
to my service. I cannot blame his choice, I have therefore taken
a French lad who cannot speak a word of English. I hope he
will turn out well. He is very useful and speaks with great
purity. He will assist us much in that language and upon
occasion can give a " petit coup de main dans la cuisine ".
His wages " entre nous " are a very trifle, for the distresses of
his Country have driven so many of these poor people out of
employ that they are glad to get bread.

In February, the task of raising the company being completed, William begged Elizabeth to send him " by return of
the Post the measure of your finger for the pledge of our
eternal affection ". " I wish you ", he continued, " to ask
your Mama whether there is any impropriety in my taking a
bed at her House till our marriage ". If that stern mistress,
propriety, would allow of this it would be for their " blended
interest " for it would save him a guinea a week. The answer
of propriety is not recorded. Three weeks later he announced
with triumph " I have bought the ring "; and at a dinner at
Lord Harrington's in London, wrote the happy bridegroom,

there were twelve of us. When the Clothe was removed Lady
H. desired every body to fill a bumper of Burgundy and that
she would give us a toast. The glasses of an enormous size
were all filled when her Ladyship gave " Mrs Harness that is
to be ".

After her earlier doubts Mrs Bigg had long ago accepted
Mr Harness as a worthy and desirable son-in-law; and a
conversation with her sister who " is so good as perfectly to
approve of our plans " gave William much satisfaction. The
long engagement was at an end, their relations were satisfied,
their house was ready for them, a small income was secure, and
Bessy married her Mr Harness at the Parish Church of Aylesbury on 3 May 1791. The ceremony was performed by the
Vicar, the Reverend Thomas Lloyd, who afterwards became
the first Bishop of Newcastle. Here is a letter from a waggish
friend of the family, written just before the wedding.

Winchendon, Thursday morning

Dear Miss,

If it is a fine day to-morrow and You should be inclin'd to walk, bend your lovely Footsteps towards Hartwell Langley that I may have the Pleasure of meeting and Honour of greeting you. Did you ever know such heavenly weather? Do you not admire it? Doesn't it exhilarate and give you Spirits? Do not you wish for its Continuance? Do you take proper advantage of it and strengthen yourself by *Exercise*? There's a *Military Word*, and doesn't that please you? I say, Bigg; I wish you had a good thousand a year. We should see you then dashing away with a Equipage unequall'd: A superb Carriage, beautiful Horses, and the *handsomest and most elegant Harness* in the world.

I hope you are all well, Yea very well: It's well if you are: Farewell.

I am

Ben Vassar

Ma's Compliments to the Family.

A letter written to Elizabeth immediately after her marriage introduces us more fully to a very well loved member of the family, Mrs Alexander Croke of Chancery Lane, known to her nephews and nieces as " Aunty Croke ".

Accept, my dear dear Betty, the most fervent wishes that a sincere and affectionate heart can offer that every possible blessing and happiness may attend you and the dear, good Man, with whom you are united, and whom I greatly esteem and have infinite satisfaction in acknowledging him my Nephew. The joy of your marriage was allayed much by your departure. I felt such a void without my Betty that I cannot describe. I rejoiced at your letter to your Mama. The fine weather, as you observe, looks propitious. A beautiful day this has been; I imagine you made your appearance at Church in the Morning. I should like to have seen my Betty in her bridal array. Your Mama has undoubtedly told you every occurrence since your departure. The attention of your Friends in congratulatory visits and notes has been very flattering.

Make my affectionate regards to Capt. Harness; you shall

both have my earnest prayers that every blessing may await you.

So William and Elizabeth set up house together. The increased income William gained from his captaincy enabled him to go on half pay and for the next two or three years—probably the happiest in his life—he was able to enjoy his married life, his home, and presently his small son and daughter. But in 1793 came the war that had threatened so long, and his keen soldiering spirit and strong sense of duty called William to the army again. New regiments were rapidly being formed to meet the national emergency, and William Harness raised his quota of men to form a company in the 80th Regiment of Foot.

Before following Mr Harness overseas some words about the Croke family would not be out of place. The ancestors of Alexander Croke had been the owners of Studley Priory since 1541, the community of nuns having been dispossessed in the previous year. The original representative of the family, who came over with Norman William, bore the name of Le Blount; but with the coming to power of the Yorkist kings, the Le Blount of the day, who had been a supporter of the Lancastrians, desired to live unnoticed, and changed his name to Croke. In the sixteenth century Sir George Croke built a chapel and almshouses and added to the old priory buildings. It was, and is, a fine country house,[1] and in her later years "Aunty Croke" looked back with some nostalgia to this beloved home. In 1805 she wrote to her young great-nephew, "We have very pretty walks around Beckley, and I often take a peep at dear old Studley from the Hill above the Village".

Mrs Croke's son, Alexander—later Sir Alexander—was a barrister-at-law. He was for three years Judge of the Admiralty Court in Nova Scotia, where his attractive villa and farm were named after the Studley at home. It was several years after her niece's wedding, though it seems appropriate to record it here, that Sarah Croke received an astonishing letter from her son. Although certainly disturbing to a mother, the letter contains a charming and unusual love story.

---

[1] The Priory has now become a guest-house.

Dear Madam,

I have to communicate to you a long history, or two, at which perhaps you may be a little surprised. There is an Arabian maxim that every man should dig a well, plant a tree. and make a babe. I should have thought myself very deficient if I had not endeavoured to do my duty accordingly. Last year I dug a new pond at Studley, upon the green, near the Blacksmith's shop. Of trees you know I have planted many, and I have now to inform you that I have not been wanting in respect to the third branch. Can you believe, my dear Mother, that it is now near four years since I entered into *the holy state*, that I am the father of a fine boy, two years and two months old, and expect a little companion to him in October? Bless me! but who is the lady? Well, you shall hear all about it. You must know then that there was a pretty little girl at Studley, whom I began with admiring as a child; as she grew older my poor heart became infected, in short, it is not much to my credit, but it was something like the story of Pamela and ended in marriage. From that time till now, my *Adelaide* has been at School, and has received the best education it has been in my power to give her, and I have the satisfaction of finding that she has profited by these opportunities, completely to my expectations, and is now as well to fit as any young ladies of her age. She writes extremely well both for matter and manner, understands French, draws extremely well, and has a little music. But what is more than all she is a girl of an excellent disposition, mild and aimable in her manner, and of good religious principles. In truth, my dear mother, after four years experience, so far from repenting of what may perhaps be thought an imprudence, were it to do again I would not hesitate one moment to take her as my beloved wife, and I have every reason to believe she has a sincere affection for me. —I hope my dear mother will forgive my not making her acquainted with this event before, and had you been in town, I should certainly have made you my first confidant, and should have hoped to have profited by your advice and friendship. But it was such a thing to enter to in a letter, and we had hopes of seeing you long before this so deferred it till we met. I am now bringing my Adelaide out into the world, and have introduced her to a few of my friends, who have been very kind. It is no longer a secret, but we do not tell anybody *who* she was. So you may tell Mrs Harness with my love, but let it go no further.

Mrs Croke appears to have received with a good grace the shock of being thus suddenly presented with a grandchild and a daughter-in-law of four years standing. Adelaide was accepted and became a well loved member of the family. She admirably filled her place in society and became the mother of eleven children. Her second son, George, succeeded his father at Studley, his elder brother, Alexander, having died at the age of 20. Another brother, John, it is believed, took Holy orders.

3

Interlude in Guernsey

DURING the months and years when William Harness was separated by the calls of his profession from his wife and children he wrote to them constantly, long, devoted, anxious letters, his mind and heart ever full of the doings and the welfare of the little family left behind at Dronfield. The first lengthy parting came at the end of 1793. William, having raised his company, was now a captain in the 80th Regiment of Foot. The household in Derbyshire consisted of Elizabeth, the 2-year-old Charles, Jane the baby, and Mrs Croke, always a loved and beneficent presence in the family. She appears to have divided her time between Dronfield and London. Elizabeth's mother, Mrs Bigg, often made another of the party.

England had not at that time recognized the French Republican Government and when, in spite of Pitt's efforts for peace, hostilities had broken out between this country and revolutionary France, the war was not unpopular. This was early in 1793. A number of new regiments were called into being, the 80th among them. Although at the beginning England had her allies—Prussia, Austria, Holland, Spain—there came a time when, as in 1940, we faced the enemy alone. In the early stages of the war the leadership of the allied countries was feeble and incapable; and while the English, like the rest of the non-revolutionary world, were filled with a certain righteous indignation at the deeds of the Republic, the French were in the grip of a new and thrilling idea that gave power and enthusiasm to their ill-equipped, ragged armies.

The 80th were ordered to join the Duke of York's army in the Netherlands, and at the end of 1793 we find them embarked at Gravesend. The regiment had as its commanding officer a temporary Lieutenant-Colonel, Lord Paget, the eldest son of the Earl of Uxbridge.

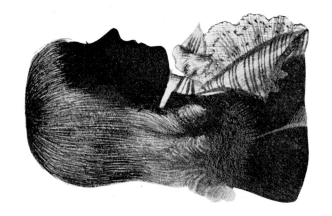

Father and Son.

An officer of the 80th.

We all dined yesterday with Lord Paget [wrote Captain Harness on Christmas Day]. He came on board in the morning and was much pleased with the order of our ship. He told me he was young at the business and begged I would give him any hints which I thought might tend to the convenience of his ship. Lord Craven and he slept on board last night. They had nothing but a blanket to wrap themselves in.

Lord Paget was a gallant, impetuous, though shrewd, young man of considerable charm, and was evidently not above learning from a junior officer who was older and more experienced. Later, as Lord Uxbridge, he was to bear a noble part in the Battle of Waterloo, where he lost a leg. What Baedeker describes as an " absurd monument to Lord Uxbridge's leg " was set in a garden next to the church in Waterloo village.[1] He it was who had raised the regiment—largely from among his father's Staffordshire tenantry. The 80th was later represented by the 2nd battalion of the South Staffordshire Regiment. Here are some of the Commanding Officer's " Conditions for young Gentlemen, above Sixteen Years Age, getting Ensigncies in Lord PAGET'S Regiment ":

You are to furnish fifteen Men for your Commission . . . and they are to be approved by the Officer commanding at Head Quarters.

No man to be under five Feet six Inches high, or upwards thirty Years old, with a good Countenance, straight, and well-made. Each Man to be carefully examined by a Surgeon before he is attested.

You are to be allowed Subsistence for each approved Man from the date of his attestation. . . . Each Recruit to furnish himself with four good Shirts, two Pair of Shoes, a Set of Brushes and Blackball, one black Stock and Clasp, two Pair of Stockings, and one Haversack, Combs and Powder Bag . . .

No Allowance whatever will be made you on Account of Deserters.

At 26, though already a Member of Parliament, representing Carnarvon Boroughs, Lord Paget might still, perhaps, be con-

---

[1] The inscription on the monument records that there lies buried the leg of the " illustrious brave and valiant " Earl of Uxbridge.

sidered one of those field officers who, as a member of the Duke of York's staff grimly put it, " are many of them boys and have attained their rank by means suggested by government at home ".[1] But he was early to prove himself a bold and inspiring leader.

A letter written four days after Christmas tells vividly of the discomforts of riding at anchor in a troopship.

> Downs, 29 December
>
> The Pilot is leaving us and we have just cast our anchor after having been five days aboard. We are strangely detained by the naval etiquette. Yesterday we waited for a convoy, to-day we cannot pass the Port-Admiral. The wind is favourable but here we must ride—sick—sick—sick! We are all very young sailors, the sea has run a little rough and has made foul work among us. Adieu! the Deal boat is alongside making villainous demands on the poor pilot.

The first stage in their campaign brought the regiment to Guernsey. While still anchored in the Downs off Deal Captain Harness wrote on 2 January 1794:

> We have waited here for a Fleet of Transports from Ostend which are now just in sight. They contain ten thousand Hessians destined for Lord Moira's army and the same convoy, the Hind Frigate, sees us all to Guernsey. Our weather is delightful, the wind quite fair, and in two days we hope to be in Guernsey.

There were, however, " all kinds of delays " in the expedition, and it was not until 11 January that William Harness wrote to his wife from Guernsey. As always, one of his first concerns was the arrival—or too often the non-arrival—of longed-for letters from home.

> The Head Quarters are at Vale Castle about three miles from the only place that can be called a Town in the Island. We have four Companies at the Castle, Lord Paget's, Lord Craven's, Major Champagné's and my own. We have estab-

---

[1] Sir Henry Calvert, quoted in *D.N.B.*

lished a comfortable but not numerous mess, it consisting of the Gentlemen above mentioned, Captain Fanchez, two young men, and the Surgeon. We ate our first dinner here yesterday. The day before the Lords, Major C. and myself met the Grandees of the place at a Major Saumarez, who has been stationed here for some years. I remained in Town on Duty that night and slept at the Hotel where Lord P. and I spent the evening tête à tête. He lent me his linnen and nightcap and, his Servant telling him he could come at but one net, he insisted upon my wearing it as he had gone without any Cap at all the night before and was quite indifferent about it. He told me he should not allow any officer to come into the Regiment whose Rank should interfere with my Promotion. He looks upon my succeeding to the Majority as certain. I shall waite a few hours for the arrival of a packet. I am sorry to find they are obliged to wait often a considerable time for a convoy and that the ready way to get letters is to suppose Guernsey a village in Devonshire and direct accordingly. I have not the exact mode of this contraband conveyance but will endeavour to possess myself compleatly with it before I finish.

The letter continues on 15 January:

Tuesday a party of us dined with a Mr Barclay. His wife is the toast of the Island very young and very handsome. In the evening we accompanyed them to the Assembly, quite a superb thing—about a hundred and fifty—few very pretty women, but very lively. Not dancing myself I went away at ten and waited at Lord P.'s till they returned to a supper he gave. Next Monday the Field Officers and Captains are asked to a dinner called the Chief Pleas Court. The troops on the Island consist of four hundred of the 78th Regiment, 600 Invalids, ourselves and about 1500 Militia. The language you know is a jargon formed from the French but most of them speak some English. Wine is very cheap, very excellent Claret at 18s. per Dozen.

Major C. has given me the following address which greatly expedites the arrival of all English communication. " Capt. Harness 80th Regt. Guernsey to the care of Mr Tozer Brixham Devon ". Let me hear often from you.

37

What depth of feeling and frustration lies in the sentence with which this letter began—a sentence comprehending many of the difficulties and delays that dogged the career of a soldier or sailor in the 1790s: " What uncertainty attends the pleasure " (and, one might add, the duty) " that is governed by the wind!" On 28 January Captain Harness received his first letter since leaving Dronfield. The packets had been delayed, not this time by the wind, but by a " fleet of French Frigates which has infested the Channel ". The direction of letters to Guernsey, Brixham, Devon, however, has proved " infinitely more expeditious ".

The stay in Guernsey lasted for many months—months during which, so many of the officers felt, opportunities were being lost through unaccountable delay.

12 February 1794

A French Marquis, his name I have forgot, dined with us yesterday; he was lamenting that we should have nothing to do, for that there never was so much dissatisfaction in France as at present and that an English army had but to land to march immediately to Paris. I find Lord Paget had asked Lord Moira to take his Regt with him; he is very warm for service, but Lord Uxbridge throws every obstacle in his way. I saw a letter from him where he says Lord M. is sorry engagements he is under to other Colonels will not permit him the flattering Honor of taking Ld P.'s Regt under his command. Yesterday a few recruits from England, one of them, who appeared to be a very pretty Lad, proved to be a woman. She had lived with a rich uncle who, she says, used her so horribly that she left him and returned to her Father's house, who, exasperated at the rash step she had taken, turned her out of Doors. She then put on man's cloathes and was going on board Ship in search of her Brother when she fell in with the Sergeant, who made her so handsome offers that she changed her plan and entered without any Bounty; it was not till she found it impossible to conceal that she acknowledged her sex.

It is not related how the military dealt with this baffling recruit. In spite of the opposition of the young Colonel's parent, rumours of possible movements were frequent and welcome.

Guernsey, 14 March 1794

I find it determined that we are to make a part of Lord Moira's Army, a circumstance that is highly gratifying to every part of the Regiment, and never, my beloved Wife, could I be employed in a service more flattering to my ambition. I shall go as first Major of Lord Paget's Regiment and as a Field Officer in the Army of Lord Moira to whom I am personally known. There is a regular communication kept up with the Royalists in Brittany and the British Coast, and it appears that the hopes of the Allied Powers have at no period of the War been more sanguine.

A new outfit involved our officer in considerable expense, but afforded him great satisfaction. In the same letter of 14 March he wrote:

I forget whether I ever told you what is our dress. The facing you know is yellow, the epaulette gold and Gold laced hat and white feather with a very handsome sword. This is the afternoon dress, in the morning we wear a Jacket, blue pantaloons to the ancles, with a border of about three inches of yellow leather and the same all up the fork, and a bearskin Helmet hat and white feather and half Boots under the pantaloons. The effect is quite what you would expect from Lord Paget's taste. It looks particularly well on Horse Back.

Was it the wearing of this dashing uniform that, a few months later, gave the proud father the idea of a winter outfit for little Charles and Jane?

1 October 1794

I hope our Children are well; poor little things, as the winter approaches I am thinking, my Betsy, you might get them some pretty little great coats of blue cloath or casimere with red collar and cuffs and some of the small 80th buttons. The buttons Mrs Croke could get from Mitchell in the Haymarket. Should they not be made with a waist and pockets behind—or to appear to have them? Consult your taste, my adored wife, and tell me the result, and, should you like theirs, you can fancy something of the kind for yourself. You will find great convenience in lining the sleeve with *silk*.

The somewhat curious idea—as it seems to us—of regimental coats for the family was rapturously received at Dronfield.

Pleased as [Charles] is, wrote Elizabeth, with the thoughts of having a little Coat, he is not half so much so as his Mama is at the idea of taking both her dear Children to walk in the Church yard the first day they wear them. I am sure they will look pretty in them, but I have begged my Aunt Croke to get them in London according to *your* directions and the measures I have sent, for I am sure there is nobody here that can make them properly. I am too anxious for them to look Regimental for to employ old Bounds, who does not know how to make a dressing Gown with proper directions. If I could have a coat myself *made properly*, you may depend I should be ready on every account to comply with your kind desire; but it would be a disgrace instead of a compliment to you and the Regiment for me to have one made ill.

What Elizabeth really wanted for herself, rather than a regimental coat, was a " riding dress ", but it is not revealed whether she acquired this. It is sad to read in a subsequent letter that " poor Jane's coat does not fit ". The price was alarming—three guineas for the two; but the buttons, Elizabeth says, " are beautiful " and " Everybody says that [Charles] looks more like you than ever ".

William had been a little worried by his small son's " timidity ", and it was with some satisfaction that Elizabeth wrote to him that this child of 2

is grown the wildest little creature that can be. I believe we need not frighten ourselves concerning his timidity. Miss Smith was here the other day for two minutes, and on meeting her he hit her a slap on the face. So you see this change requires correction.

In the early weeks of his sojourn in the island William had been much occupied with the possibility of changing his captaincy for a majority. Lord Paget was as good as his word and determined that Harness should succeed to the next vacant post. While he was eager for this advancement and fully conscious of the advantage that it would bring him, there was to be weighed against it the question of the paymastership that he held, an office which added considerably to his income. The thought that in becoming a major he would have to give up this source of revenue made the decision a very hard one for William. The final determining factor was the financial value of the commission. " You are not ", he wrote to Elizabeth, " for giving up the paymastership, but the other thing would be so infinitely better and in value two thousand pounds higher than my Company; so that you see altho' the income is less the property is greater." It was therefore as a major that William Harness eventually landed in the Low Countries. It appears that he got off easily, as he paid a mere £500 for his elevation. " My Majority ", he wrote in May, " is dated the 19th December, about the time I left you. Little did we think at that time of the speedy good fortune that awaited us."

Life on the island during those lingering months was far from dull, judging by the frequent mention of dinners, dances, assemblies, and a " levy " of the Lieutenant-Governor. Captain Harness was for his day one of the most temperate of men. Nevertheless on one occasion he wrote, somewhat shame-facedly, of what can only be described as an orgy. The immediate cause of this festivity was a victory of Sir John Warren, a distinguished officer who, after a curious early career, alternating between the navy and Cambridge (where he took his M.A. in 1776), made his final choice for the navy at the age of 24. William Harness was well acquainted with Sir John. In March 1791 he had written to Elizabeth, " I dined on Saturday with Sir John Warren, whose friendship does not seem to have lessened from our absence." Sir John was now in command of a squadron of frigates in the Channel. They were on the lookout for a French squadron which was doing much damage to English trade. On 23 April 1794 he fought a successful action with four French frigates, and captured three of them. It was this exploit that formed the occasion for the jollification a few days later.

Guernsey, 6 May 1794

I am tempted to give you an account of a dinner I gave here last week, but fear you will think me drunken and dissipated. You well know me. Lord Paget, Count Rice (whose trial Mrs Bigg will remember), Colonel Champagné &c &c—in short we were nine sat down. We had just received intelligence of the particulars of Sir John Warren's action (for it was heard by us all) and the Spirits it gave contributed to the shocking business. At a proper time after dinner from the chair I gave " Sir John and his Squadron ". Lord P. said they each deserved a Bumper; they were severally drunk. The Duke of York's Gazettes were brought and we finished three dozen of Claret besides Port and Madeira. Lord P. was put into my bed, Count Rice was found in the morning in a ditch. Colonel Champagné found his way home without a hat or Scabbard to his Sword, Captain Forster and Captain Rooke rode off to Town five miles from their quarter. But my Bessy blushes for me. We had a field day in the morning and the Band was left here; all contributed to the shameful scene. You once saw me in the same situation. I trust it cannot happen a third time.

Count Rice was tryed at Salisbury, I think for shooting the Vicomte du Borré at Bath;[1] it made much noise. He is an extremely able man. He is here as Mr Clarke, having changed his name for the better security of his neice and Sister, who are at Paris. He is to have a Corps of Emigrants and is the particular friend of the Marquis du Dresnay, who was lately here and who has the Command of all the incorporated emigrés.

We hear more of this pleasant Frenchman in a letter written at the end of August when the Regiment was preparing to leave the island.

Our companies are just embarked. The Compte de Rice has just left me. We have lived in intimacy. His understanding

[1] The two following verses are taken from a ballad dated Bath, 18 May 1803:

Just take me up to yonder Down,
   Where Count du Barry fell
Whose death I've heard old Father John
   Times out of number tell.

How did he fall? With one, Count Rice
   Through cards, or jealous dread,
He quarrell'd—and went there to fight
   Rice shot du Barry dead!

is of the first rate and I have been delighted as often as I have seen him. He has this day opened to me in confidence much of the plans of the Prince's, has shewn me letters which prove that no material step is taken without his approbation. Should the expedition intended land in Brittany *I shall hold an appointment* which, if crowned with the success the plan seems to merit will give me an *immense fortune* and influence. You will read this with surprize. I am very anxious to get forward in my French, for I feel that I shall be able to do the cause most essential service at the time I am securing a fortune for ourselves. He says he has great confidence in my Honor and clear judgement, and has entrusted me with secrets of much importance. My Bessy, how unlike myself am I writing; really it is not vanity that urges on my Pen, but the desire I have that our ideas of future happiness should run in the same current.

What this affluent appointment was to be we shall never know, for " the success the plan seems to merit " was never achieved. Elizabeth's comment on the " shocking business " was mildness itself. " The account you give of your dinner ", she wrote, " is not quite in the stile of my H., but you account for its ending as it did. No, I never yet blushed for my most beloved friend, and I know him too well to suppose I shall ever have cause to do it."

William was afraid that in his absence Elizabeth, like so many mothers of young children, was becoming too much engrossed in her own home affairs. There are tact and tenderness and good common sense in a letter written from Guernsey on 14 March 1794.

I hope the Biscoes promise to make good. You tell me they do not expect you to call on them. You mean perhaps against your inclination or convenience, but it is civility due to all Strangers, and however retired my Bessy may wish to live it is what you owe yourself to call or leave your name, and this will give an opening for better neighbourhood whenever you please to change your mode of living. But my tenderly dear wife for my sake do not seclude yourself from the little society in your power. Believe me nothing can give me severer pain than to know you debar yourself of any of the few amusements within your reach. I feel the delights you must experience in *our own Children*—but my adored and everbeloved wife, the mind is of too inflexible a texture to admit us to take up and cast off habits at pleasure, and should you by seclusion once lose the relish for society it will be difficult to recover a proper taste for it, or mix in it with ease. This observation I have drawn from my own feelings, for occupied with those interests which are never strange to my imagination, the little desire I had for enterring into this society betrayed me into frequent rudenesses; nor was it till I had been some time on the Island and my Friends had remarked this insensibility that I began to discover that my character as a Gentleman required a closer attention to the *duties* of society.

Needless to say, Elizabeth did call, and the Biscoes became kind and valued friends.

A gala day in Guernsey was a certain Monday in May when the regimental colours were consecrated. Captain Harness evidently expected trouble with his men before the day was over, but all went well, owing probably to the interposition of the rain. He sent his wife what he rather unjustly describes as " a very flat account of a scene that was highly interesting ".

Guernsey, 29 May 1794

Last Monday our Colours were consecrated. So very unusual a ceremony attracted the whole Island; it was really a fine sight. The Regiment was drawn up in a square, the Field Officers mounted with Horse Furniture, the Governor attended and all the fashion of the Island. The Colours were in a Marquee near. The Adjutant brought the Colours to the Governor, the Men presented their Arms, the Governor saluted the Colours and presented them to Lord Paget. On his dismounting he saluted them, and received them most gracefully. He presented them to the Regiment, marching with one in each hand up the center of the square, the Drums and fifes all beating a point of War [1] and our excellent Band playing God save the King. He gave them to the Ensigns and

---

[1] Probably a charge; cf. French, *faire pointe*—to make a charge.

44

mounted. He began a most beautiful and manly speech by saying that the King had done him the Honor to present him with these colours; that he felt the Honor and the duty of so sacred a Gift; that in executing this trust he knew he had but to present them to His Regiment, who would support them with their lives in defence of so gracious a Soveriegn and in guarding the Honor, the laws, the religion and the prosperity of their Country. " From you they never will receive a stain and as long as I command you I shall feel confident and happy." The whole gave three chears, the Music and Drums struck up, the Ensigns marched with the Colours round the square, each Officer saluting them as they past. The Governor then gave a speech congratulating the Men on their Officers and the Officers on the Men, and both and their Country on that day. The Chaplin then gave a Prayer for the Regiment and a Sermon. The Men were then placed in line and the Colours in the Center, when they were ordered to pile their Arms and were marched by Companies to ten large Tables, one for each Company, the whole forming a large square, where was provided for them 1500 pounds of roast beef, 1000 pounds of plumb pudding, a thousand pounds of bread, a thousand pounds of Potatoes and 1200 quarts of ale. The Officers, Ladies &c &c went to a very large Tent and partook of a very excellent colation, with strawberries, Cherries and all sorts of good things. The effect was awful and grand in the business of the consecration. Lord Paget's speech from his rank, his Person, his situation with us and from the affectionate and graceful Manner of his utterance could not fail of powerful impression. The Governor shed tears. In his speech he said he had seen Lord P.'s father, then a Brother Captain of Grena-diers, lead his Company into action; he was the witness of his coolness and congratulated the Regiment on their leader, his Son. Lord Paget gave an excellent dinner, of course on that occasion very crowded, and the wine could not be for-gotten. I feared the conclusion. After the Men had dined it began to rain most violently. I never was so wet, it continued for hours. I drew off my detachment and, instead of sending them by an Officer, marched home with them myself, trusting in my wet jacket to excuse me, and escaped a day I had dreaded for several days before.

In the intervals of his busy life on the island Captain Harness found time to send off presents of yellow carnation plants and Guernsey lilies to various friends; and to his Bessy, with many directions for their proper care, he entrusted " two Pipes of admirable Port ", some of which was to provide presents for their neighbours. " The remainder will put it in our power always to have good port by us." How life came to be so busy was explained when William apologized for the brevity of some of his letters.

23 May 1794

When I tell you that the Paymaster of the 78th is excused all other Duties from the weight of business attached to it in a new Regiment, and that the difficulties attending that Office in this, from the very great hurry in which it was raised, are much greater, and that I have the charge of one of the most important Posts in the Island added to it, as well as the disciplining the young Troops, you will see, my ever adored wife, that the dearest wishes of my heart are at times those I am obliged first to defer.

Servant trouble appears from time to time in his correspondence.

12 February 1794

James is too young to have much method and too much tempted not sometimes to fail. Of course he cannot make a perfect substitute for my faithful Thomas; but he has many good points, he is *sober* and listens to me when I have occasion to scowld him. He is improved in waiting at table, but he is not clean in his person, nor does he always find out the time I usually dress at. Yesterday I dined at Lord P.'s house, where he had a party; we dine here at five. I sent James to Town on a message at eleven, and he returned, I am told, at 7 in the evening. Another day he had got drunk with Lord P.'s Servants, staid out all night, had the Keys of my Rooms in his pocket. I came home late, very wet, was obliged to break open the doors, found no fire and my bed as I had left it in the morning. He confesses his faults but is unused to drink wine, which they insist on his doing, and it gets the better of him. You see what bad examples he has to contend with.

James's understanding and long-suffering master did his best
to help the young man; for, unlike some officers of his day,
William Harness was full of thought and solicitude for the
comfort of his soldiers. They are " our poor Fellows ", " our
gallant Fellows ", or, occasionally, when there has been an
outbreak of looting, " our Villains ". Elizabeth wrote of a
" poor Recruit " who had been to call on her: " He said that
he had seen you a fortnight before, that he had been in the
Hospital, that you never came to the Town without calling
on him, that you had behaved as Father to him."

Harness was much concerned about the men's water supply.

6 May 1794

Lord Paget dined with me yesterday and I mentioned that
the Water was very bad, and wished him to make application
to the Governor for a Water Cart to fetch it from some excellent
Springs at about a mile and a half distance, and from which
I have had all the Water for my own use. It is perhaps a
little vanity that leads me to send my own Bessy the Order in
consequence, to show how ready and flattering attention has
been paid to my representation. I am constituted to receive
much satisfaction from circumstances of this nature, and the
most soothing alleviation furnished me for your absence is the
hope that I am contributing to the health and Comfort of
those entrusted to my care. We may be said to be unusually
healthy, but I have availed myself of the death of a fine
young Grenadier (for that Company is with us) to strengthen
my application.

Lord Paget's order ran:

Headquarters, 6 May 1794
General Orders

The water at Le Hommet being deemed unwholesome and
reported by Major Harness of the 80th Regmt Commanding
at that Post to have occasioned Illness of a dangerous nature
amongst the detachment stationed there, to avert the possibility of unhealthiness to the Troops from any avoidable cause,
and to obviate the present apprehension, the Acting Deputy
Quarter Master General is directed to order a carriage to be

constantly plied at Le Hommet for the purpose of conveying Water to the Garrison there, from the best and most wholesome Springs in the adjacent District.

That the young Commanding Officer also had the welfare of his men truly at heart is shown by an unusual test that he underwent. Major Harness (as he had now become), as befitted a somewhat older man, was more cautious.

8 April 1794

Lord Paget and Mr Rooke (a Son of the General's at Woodstock) are living for a week on Soldier's fare for the experiment. They asked me to join them, but as our Mess is a very excellent one, and no immediate necessity prompts the trial, I feared the effects of so slender diet and water at this season of the year in a spot that's remarkably aguish.

During her husband's absence Elizabeth planned to visit her brother-in-law's family at Wickham. There were some slight difficulties in the way. One was connected with William Harness's new military dignity. "Our sweet Children, they must go with me. I cannot leave either behind, but the misfortune of it is I then cannot do without Mary, for the appearance of a *Major's Lady* and two Children without a Servant would be shocking." The journey was accomplished, however, after the Major had made out a route for the travellers. Elizabeth evidently felt that her wardrobe needed some attention before she faced her sister-in-law.

We had a parcel from my Aunt Croke. You know I was in absolute want of a new hat or bonnet; I begged my Aunt to send me a straw one. She has sent a hat trim'd in a pretty plain manner with green Ribbon. I know that is yr favorite colour and I have tried it on twenty times, and vext that it does not become [me], because I hope my H. will see me in it. She has sent Charles a Soldier to fight the French with should they dare to come to D[ronfield].

In June Guernsey had a taste of real warfare.

Guernsey, 23 June 1794

On Witsunday I was awoke about half past six by an Officer running naked into my Room, exclaiming that two Fleets were at that moment warmly engaged off the Island. I hastened on my Cloaths and ran downstairs, when I saw eight ships firing very smartly at each other. At that time, not being able to discern our Friends from our Enemies, I instantly despatched my orderly Dragoon with the intelligence to the Governor and hoisted my Flag as a signal of the approach of an Enemy's Fleet. The action became warmer and the Ships coming nearer and nearer till we could discover the Crescent, the Druid and the Eurydice, bearing the weight of fire of five immense large French Frigates, three of which had been 74s cutt down. The scene was more interesting than you can conceive; the Balls we saw strike throw the Ships and dash into the Sea. At one time three of the Enemy were firing at once on the Crescent, we had every apprehension for her. At the time I received Orders to give His Majesty's Ships every succour from our Great Guns at the Batteries and, should the Enemy approach near enough for our small arms to take effect, to annoy him with them too. A Company of Guernsey artillery joined me, our Guns were loaded and every preparation made. The Crescent tacked and past the French squadron, received the Broad side of three of them. She then ran in so close to us, chased by the Enemy, that we could almost jump on board. She was within the rocks and our fears from these dreadful Enemies too increased; but she past most ably through them, having a Guernsey Man and the most skilful pilote of the Island on board. By this manoeuvre he gave time to the other Frigates to escape and in the afternoon we had the satisfaction of seeing them all safe in Port. Two Guns were fired from the shore, but at the other side of the Bay, and when, from their direction, it was impossible they could carry effect. The Action was most masterly managed on the Part of our Frigates; it must have been highly flattering to Sir James Saumarez, who is a Guernsey man, with all this part of the Island bearing testimony of his Seamanlike Conduct. It formed a sight that seldom occurs. Happening immediately off my Post, where from the elevated Ground every movement, almost of a rope, could be discerned, from the very superior Force of the Enemy, from the part I might be every minute called to bear in it, as a Soldier I had an interest, as an Englishman I had fears and as a Man my hopes and fears were in constant motion; for the Flames, the explosion of broadsides, the Balls striking and playing along the surface of the Sea altogether formed one of the most magnificent spectacles the Human mind could contemplate. We sent off a boat during the action with a Pilote, not knowing our Friends were so well provided; our men were all most all petitioning me to let them go on board. The French Ships were very fine ones, their tricolour Flags and Pendents were flying, but so confused and mistaken were their Signals that some of their Ships had nearly fifty Flags hoisted at the same time. As a spectacle the grandeur of that day will not be easily effaced.

By 21 July the Buffs, the 63rd, and 88th Regiments had left the Channel Islands.

Lord Paget is very uneasy that the 88th should be ordered on Service and his Regiment left at home. Indeed his Spirits are much affected by it. The system of the War is likely to be changed and our destination may depend upon it. How perfidious a part have our Allies taken! In the commencement of the War we could be considered as little else but auxiliaries to those Powers that have now forsaken us. Europe at this moment appears at a great crisis. The past presents a speaking lesson.

The restless young Commanding Officer was off on an expedition of his own.

Lord Paget is gone to look along the French Coast in La Nymphe, who sailed on Saturday in search of some French Trade Ships seen off. Lord Paget is amazingly fond of the Navy and, dining on board when these Orders were received, the temptation of a two days cruise was too powerful to be resisted. He every day gives better claims to prudence than can be asserted for him on this occasion.

At last the regiment was on the move. Before he left Guernsey William Harness sent his wife some good advice.

Guernsey, 27 August 1794

In quitting this place the only thing I have to regret is the interruption it is possible I may sometimes find in hearing from my most dearly beloved Wife; but this I hope we shall contrive remedies for. For the rest we have the Guardianship of Heaven, to whom, instead of fearful mistrust, our gratitude is due. My Bessy will shew that love for me that I shall prize above Worlds; and with a cheerfulness shall I go through the duties of my station I could not feel were I to reflect that the woman on earth I have ever loved most faithfully gave way to gloomy and fruitless apprehensions she would hate me did I myself submit to. They are unworthy of us both. Nothing, trust me my Bessy, is more aimable in either sex than submitting with beautiful propriety to every dispensation of Heaven. That, on certain occasions it is possible may occur, the wife who tenderly loves me should feel a solicitude is to give me a testimony of her affection; but this will ever be corrected by the influence of a sound judgment and a right understanding, or it dwindles into the snivelling of vulgar and little characters.

The regiment was held up for two or three weeks at Deal owing to the presence of French ships in the neighbourhood, which necessitated waiting for a larger convoy. From Deal Major Harness was able to send home another addition to the cellar.

Deal, 9 September 1794

I have ordered six Dozen of Hock, sent on board my Ship by my Friend, Le Compte de Rice, to be landed here and forwarded on to you, as it is not a good campaigne wine, and his extreme kindness has furnished me with all sorts of good things against the climate.

The safe landing and forwarding of the gift was attended by some difficulty.

15 September

The Hock is gone off this morning. I found it impossible to enter it at the custom house here (on account of its being in bottles) till a representation of this informality had been made

51

to the Commissioners in London. This would have induced a delay that might have given a great uncertainty of its coming to you safe. I hope there is [safety] in the mode I have adopted in despatching it without any formality at all; but this will remain a secret between ourselves and I shall be glad to hear of it getting safely to you.

Now I am on Wine, I presume you have gotten the pipes of port. No 2 should be filled up with some of Number 1 when you draw it off, but previously No 1 should be clearifyed by about a dozen and a half whites of eggs, about five weeks before bottling, and stopped up close. Let your corks be the best that can be procured. I paid Sixty Guineas for the two pipes at Guernsey. In packing I find dry sand is preferred to saw dust, and that very sparingly, just to fill up the chasm made by the bottles not being of the same shape. The utmost attention is required in seeing the bottles clean and *dry*. I think, my beloved wife, I have dismissed this subject which, important as it is, I almost grudge the space it contains on this paper.

The port had arrived safely at Hull. From thence it came by canal to Chesterfield and was brought by waggon to Dronfield. Its arrival caused some domestic upheaval and much anxious consultation with neighbours.

The Pipes of Port [wrote Elizabeth] are arrived safe and are placed in the little Hall. I had no idea you meant it to be bottled yet, for Mr Greenway said it should stand a twelve-month. At all events the Hen House would not be a safe situation for it. They stand on logs of wood some distance from the Ground, and are as well situated as if in a cellar that is *not arched*. They will be covered with straw and matting as soon as Mr Hill has been here again. Mr Hill and Mr Dell frightened me by saying it would certainly be spoilt unless it was in an arched cellar or bottled off. Mr Greenway was so good to be here when it came. He advised me to have Wildgoose here in case of an accident. There were seven Men in all, the two Pearsons, Hobson a bricklayer, Wildgoose and *his Man*, and Mr Smith desired Pearson would call on his servant. They had bread and cheese and Ale; 'twas hard work. Wildgoose had a shilling for his trouble, which Hobson was very angry at and said he would do twelve times as much for nothing. I paid Pearson for the carriage twelve shillings.

We hear just a year later that " 15 Dozen of Magnum Bonum bottles " had been ordered from Rotherham. William's letter of 15 September continued:

This dreadful delay is the ruin of our Regiment, confined as they are in close Transports. The Mary and Elizabeth is a shocking Ship; she has been in the service all the War, is but lately returned from the West Indies. Our poor Fellows have a nasty Fever broken out amongst them and I have prevailed upon Lord P. to take all the Men in health out of her. In consequence I have removed to the John. I hope by this timely arrangement the health of our Men will be preserved and that of the Sick restored. Forty were taken ill in two days. The Surgeon is removed to her and he tells me this morning that most of the Sick are better. My own health, my Bessy will learn with pleasure, was never better.

Meanwhile Lord Paget was off on another expedition. In view of the proximity of the French fleet it is not surprising that his absence caused his officers some anxiety.

Seven Ships, including the Admiral's and our Convoy, are gone out this morning in chase of an equal number of French ones. Lord Paget is gone with Captain Durham. We are very anxious to see them return with two or three of the French Men in tow.

18 September 1794

The signal for sailing is now flying and as I fold up this paper I must hasten on board. Lord Paget is not returned but Admiral Payton has ordered the Venus for our Convoy, the wind is perfectly fair and we hope to be in Flushing to-morrow.

Arrived at Flushing, Major Harness wrote on 22 September, " Lord Paget has not yet joined us but is chasing the French Frigates in the North Sea "; and on 1 October, when the 80th was on board a transport—the *John*—in the East Scheldt, " We have not seen Lord Paget or heard from him. He will be very sorry for his cruize." A day or two later the lovable, erratic young Colonel returned.

Thursday

Lord Paget surprized us this morning. He had heard nothing of the regt, had arrived at Flushing last evening and taken a small boat for Dort. He has had a miserable time of it having weathered three gales of wind. They had stretched away into the North Sea and were separated by the weather. They had frequent intelligence of the French Squadron from Vessells they spoke, but never saw them. We hope to reach Dort in two tides but the wind is so contrary we are obliged to anchor when the tide will not serve. Lord P. meant to remain with us, but I urged him to go forward and stop the march of the Troops till we come up.

The letter concludes with words of encouragement to an anxious wife.

I am told I shall receive very considerable premiums on my Bills, and I indulge the soul gratifying hope of returning with a Comfortable Income to pass in blissful ease my every future hour with you, my Angel, in mutual love and in joint endeavors to present to the world our Children, as aimable, as good, and as polished as our wishes could make them. I am told Major Armstrong is getting the Lt Colonelcy of a new Regt, which will make me the first Major. Again I must not cease urging you to keep up your Spirits. You know what an enemy dejection is to good looks, and what would be my anguish to see yours gone! For my sake preserve with every care a form I doat on, the dwelling of a heart I live but for. Distance magnifys danger in a greater degree than it diminishes real bodies, and mole hills at a little distance are formed into Mountains, and again removed become monsters of alarm and horror. I fear my Bessy from a love of me will but too often alarm herself with dangers I never know, and this idea is the most painful one I have to go through. A Campagne in this delightful Country for an Officer of my Rank furnishes much instruction, much to amuse the mind in its progress, with almost every comfort, at a risk which when compared to that of the subaltern Ranks becomes contemptible.

4

The Low Countries

THE CAMPAIGN in Holland with the 30-year-old Duke of York, King George's second son, as Commander-in-Chief, was going far from well. The young Duke was not unlearned in his profession, having studied the science of arms at Berlin under the eye of Frederick the Great. At the time of the Dutch campaign he was a leader of cool, unimaginative courage and practical knowledge, but lacking in resourcefulness and somewhat slow of brain. And he was badly let down by his allies. Yet although at times he made grave mistakes, he was to become, in many ways, an excellent Commander-in-Chief, with real concern for the welfare of the rank and file of his men. He initiated several reforms and, without abolishing the system of buying commissions in the army, he mitigated the scandal by increasing the number of unpaid promotions; and he suppressed the granting of commissions to children. He founded the Duke of York's School for soldiers' children and was responsible for the establishment both of the Royal Military College and of the Staff College.

A few days after arriving in Holland Major Harness went to Rotterdam to get money for the regiment, and from there he wrote:

10 October 1794

We are at present at Bommell [1] but expect every day orders to quit it. From the steeple we not only see the Town of Bois-le-Duc but the Shells absolutely fall into it. We are for a week at Bommell which expires the day after to-morrow, when we cross the Wahal and take post in the Villages on *this side* of it. We have the Meuse at present between the Enemy and

[1] Zalt Bommel, an attractive and historic little town on the south bank of the Waal.

us. The night before last they took possession of Fort St André, a small Island between that of Bommel and Bois-le-Duc. Our Post is not considered as tenable and it is supposed the Island,[1] which is of great importance, will be given up. Two thirds of the Dutch are disaffected. The enemy in consequence are in possession of every intelligence. The Duke is drawing off his army into Winter Quarters. The season is very wet and the Men becoming extremely sickly. We have three hundred in the Hospital. I had the good fortune to bring in the John without a sick man. I have excellent Quarters at Bommel. We hear the Enemy on the other side of the River. The Cannonade at Bois-le-Duc is very heavy. As soon as we get into Winter Quarters I shall, I hope, be at liberty to pass a month with you and our sweet Children. General Balfour commands the district we occupy. We make the Right of the Duke's army.

That same day, 10 October, Bois-le-Duc surrendered. The British Government sent a warning to the Dutch that unless they exerted themselves more the British army would be withdrawn from Holland. The week that was to be spent at Bommel lengthened out into over a fortnight and on 23 October the regiment was still there. So far their experience of the war had, at any rate for the officers, not been too uncomfortable and the relations with the enemy were apparently of the pleasantest.

We live well and the Officers have but little to do. The Enemy have left this part of the Country, which is become very strong. In the neighbourhood of Fort St André a few shots have been every day exchanged at the working Parties. These are Captains' Commands composed of the 78th and 80th. Two men of the 78th were wounded three days ago by the discharge of Grape shot among them. This was occasioned by a Drunken Grenadier of ours insulting them. It is wonderful how very handsomely they act. They offer all kinds of things to our Soldiers. They talk to us in the civilest way in the world.[2] A Captain crossed the water the other day and came to see us;

---

[1] Presumably the Bommeler Waert, a tongue of land, very nearly an island, between the Waal and the Meuse. The narrow entrance to the east was defended by Fort St André.

[2] " Their civility makes me do all but forget their late atrocities ", wrote Elizabeth in her reply.

after talking some time he returned. They told us that they had taken a British Regiment, which we find but too true. The 37th formed an advanced Corps to the Duke's Army; Major Hope commanded them. He saw the Enemy in great force marching down upon him. He wrote to the Adjutant General for Orders; the Adjutant General was gone to the Hague and his Servant put the letter in his Pocket to give when he returned. Major Hope considered that he could not retreat without orders and in a short time the Regiment found themselves surrounded by the Enemy's Cavalry. A good proportion are said to have suffered and our accounts say the Major alone escaped by leaping over a wide Ditch.

On Sunday Colonel Barnard came to me; he said Lord Newark had exchanged into his Regiment with Lord Craven under the idea of quitting the Service, and that if I would accept of the Lt-Colonelcy at the regulated price he would recommend me to the Duke for it. Conceive, my Bessy, how much I was struck with so very kind an offer. He told me that Sir William Clarke and himself had from the beginning of this business had their Eye upon me for the Lieut-Colonelcy. He gave me two days to consider of it. Captain Ford offered me as much for my present Majority as I should give for the Lt-Colonelcy. My Bessy will perhaps hear with surprize that I refused this very flattering mark of Col. Barnard's kindness. I sometimes condemn myself for the Part I have taken. I wrote to him that my Prospects in the 80th must be very dazzling and my situation in it highly advantageous when they could tempt me to decline serving so very eligibly in the 84th. On the score of income I should be giving up most seriously. The 80th will not most probably be reduced; the chances are against the 84th. It is not impossible but I may get the Lt-Colonelcy of this Regiment without purchase, as Col. J. Champagné is likely to get that of an old Regiment. In short I hope I have done right, there is much on both sides to puzzle. Our dear Children may be the better for my keeping about Lord Paget. I told him my attachment to his Regiment would not let me quit it even for promotion. We continue dreadfully sickly, having four hundred unfit for Duty, including two hundred left in the General Hospital at Dort. Those Dye daily. It is a melancholy thing.

57

We have just got Orders to march for Arnhem. His Grace is wonderfully unpopular " entre nous "; being with him we shall always be the first to fly. He is seldom within ten miles of the Enemy.

The last sentence appears scarcely to do justice to one who, whatever the faults of his private life, was a brave, honourable, hardworking soldier. Sir John Fortescue wrote of the Duke's achievement as Commander-in-Chief, " in 1795 he took over a number of undisciplined and disorganised regiments, filled for the most part with the worst stamp of man and officer, and . . . in less than seven years he converted these unpromising elements into an army." [1]

By the beginning of November the 80th were taking a more active part in the war.

Nymegen, 2 November 1794

We remained two days at Arnhem and proceeded to this Town, where we arrived yesterday. At the former place the Duke of York received us graciously. He came up with us on the march and, as I was in the rear, he addressed himself to me and rode in close conversation for a mile. I dined with him and was presented to Prince William of Gloucester [2] and had the Honor to sit next to him at Table. He was on the Duke's right Hand and Lord Paget on the other. We had expected that we were to rest at Arnhem, being sent there to give time to our sick to recover, but the Duty of this Town was so severe on the Garrison that it was found necessary to relieve a part of it. It is a good Town, very strongly fortified but the works are so extensive that it will become necessary to strengthen the Garrison. The French tryed a few shots but found they did not reach half way to the Town. They have no heavy artillery, our Batteries keep playing upon them. The Weather is most unfavourable to them; it has rained almost incessantly for the last four days and must oblige them to retire. I am very comfortably lodged. We have an excellent Coffee House where everybody meets. Nothing can be more

---

[1] *A History of the British Army*, Vol. 4, *1789-1801*, 1906, Bk. XII, p. 929.

[2] Nephew of George III, who served in the First Regiment of Foot Guards during the Flanders Campaign. He was a prince not of great intelligence, but of high moral character. Much of his income was spent in charity.

sociable. But for the Guns from our Batteries I should scarce know I am in a Garrison Town, but it is dreadfully hard upon the poor fellows, as very strong Picquets are obliged to be kept day and night unprotected from the weather and not permitted to light fires lest they should attract the fire of the Enemy. These Picquets are Captains' Parties in which I have no part, and I have all sorts of clever things to keep off the rain. Notwithstanding the severe rain of yesterday I found myself perfectly dry on my arrival. I have four Horses, two of them carry my Trunks, one with hampers of Wine and porter and cold meat, and soup which I make into a jelly, and by cutting a piece out can immediately warm a bason. Wherever I go I find every kind of civility from the Dutch-men upon whom we are billetted. It is chiefly in the best Houses and most of them speak French.

5 November

While I was writing an Order came for us to march in the night to cross the river Linge and waite for orders—that the Garrison was retreating. We marched, we remained under arms till the next night at twelve o'clock when we were order'd to return to this Town. Last night we were under arms. A sorti was made from the Garrison, the Gazette will give you the account. When I have a moment's leisure I will give it you more correct, but the post is going out. I am quite well; the fatigue of the last three days has been great. In the morning we quit the Town for a Village between this and Arnhem. I believe this Town must be given up.

A letter written from Elst, the village, half-way between Nymegen and Arnhem, to which the regiment withdrew, tells of the exciting and difficult evacuation of Nymegen and, alas, of the excesses that accompanied it.

10 November 1794

We have been two days at this Village, which the Buffs and 80th took possession of, on the evacuation of Nimmegen. You probably will see the account of that event before this letter reaches you. The place was found untenable, all the communication we had with this side the Country being by a temporary bridge of Boats, which was commanded by the

French Batteries and which it was impossible to prevent them destroying. Their Guns were opened on it the morning we came away and one of the boats were then sunk. Two of our Men were wounded in crossing it, and no sooner were we on this side of it, than we were ordered back again into the Town. We were all that day on the lines, the Enemy throwing shells from all points into the Town. By the Evening many Houses were totally destroyed, several were on fire, and few had totally escaped damage; the Bridge had suffered materially. At this time there were fifteen Brittish Regiments in the Town besides Cavalry and a strong force of Dutch and Hanoverians, all shut up without the power of acting, and who must have inevitably surrendered had the bridge taken fire, which we had every reason to apprehend, as it seemed to be the grand object to which the French directed their attention. About Ten o'clock the Garrison took the advantage of the night and began to move from the Town, the bridge having been replaced by planks in the best manner the moment would allow. By morning all the Brittish off Duty had crossed. In passing throw the Town the miseries of the poor Inhabitants were very affecting, who had not only their present misfortunes and future fears from the Enemy to sustain, but they saw themselves shamefully robbed and abused, and their Houses plundered by what ought to have been their protectors. A Lady running from her house, which had just been struck by a shell, had her Ear-ring pulled from her Ear by one of our Villains. A Soldier of the 28th run into the next house and robbed a poor Woman of Twenty Guildres. The excesses of our Army are truly horrible. During the following night all the Troops left the Town except a Dutch Regiment, which were on board a Vessell serving as a Bridge, when her main-mast was shot away and the French, who were then entering the Town, dragged the Vessell in and the Regiment was taken. We left between eighty and ninety pieces of heavy artillery and an immense quantity of ammunition. In short Nimmegen seems to be another Dunkirk.[1] The Army now occupy the Villages on the

---

[1] At this earlier Dunkirk evacuation, which took place at the beginning of September, the Duke had successfully extricated his forces under cover of night, when it had seemed that they must be cut off. As in 1940 an immense quantity of war stores had to be abandoned.

left [1] Bank of the Waal and are busy in erecting works to prevent the Enemy crossing that River. It is broad and rapid, and of course extremely difficult it must be found to transport an Army over it in the face of an Enemy. But I understand from General Fox that our present position is not to be of long duration as this side the Country cannot be preserved when powerfully attacked—and the lateness of the season make a winter quarter indispensible to a harrassed and sickly army. Our people were out three nights together without the smallest shelter whatever. Elst is a large Village. I occupy a Gentleman's House, his Gardens, Stables and every part is in our possession. The Soldiers are in the Barns and out houses. I do everything to restrain abuses, and hope in some degree succeed. My health, my dearest wife, is extremely good. Every kind of provision is in the utmost plenty as everything is brought to market for security. There is a report that the Dutch are negotiating a separate peace and have agreed to a cessation of arms for a fortnight. I cannot vouch for the truth, and conceive the cessation nugatory, as, with the French on the other side the River, during that period, they can only prepare for action.

On 17 November the 80th was still at Elst and expecting to remain there for some time " as the present object is to prevent the Enemy from crossing the Waal ". It was distressing to find that " the exchange which was lately so much in favor of England is fallen six per Cent below par ".

We have a strong idea that the army will return to England; it is supposed that our possessions will be strongly Garrisoned and that the War on our part will become defensive. The next month must determine, as I believe every thinking man in the army is sensible of the impossibility of carrying on the War in this Country. The Enemy yesterday sent a flag to say that the decree of giving no quarter was annulled and that Officers who are taken Prisoners will receive pay according to their Rank. This was never before formally notifyed although the former part of the Message has been long understood.

[1] Surely Major Harness means the right bank.

The regiment appears to have fallen again into comparative quiet, though it had not yet reached the desired winter quarters. There is no further news until 2 December, when they were at Zandwyke, close to Tiel, a town on the Waal between Bommel and Nymegen. At Zandwyke they were " cantoned in about eight houses, the men occupying the very large Barns which Holland is famous for ".

Lord Paget wishing to lodge in Tiel, the Colonel Champagnés have the House allotted for him, and I with the four nearest Companies to me have the most distant Quarter. It fortunately (as it generally happened) is an excellent house belonging to a Gentleman who lives in Tiel, who has fitted up in a very pretty style the part now occupied by me, as a Summer residence. Lord Paget being desirous to be in the same Brigade with his Brother, we have been appointed to the sixth and marched in consequence to our present Quarters to join it. We had hoped to have found a winter Quarter, in one of the large Towns but the defence of the Waal being the present object it is not expedient to withdraw the Troops from its banks. The greater part of the French army we understand are gone into Winter Quarters. We are told from respectable authority that they have now sixty thousand sick in Hospitals. We furnish a chain of Picquets, but nothing can be more quiet than this neighbourhood. Several Officers are going home of other Regiments, and some of ours begin to look out for leave, but most of us judge it more advantageous to defer asking leave till we are assured that we are to remain in this Country, a circumstance that seems almost impossible, considering the present dispositions of our allies and the actual state of things as well at home as upon this Continent. The Dutch it is said are determined upon a peace, it appears to me as certain as geometric truth could make it that we must be in England in two months. Anxious as I am, my adored wife, to fly to you, I cannot but think I am doing right, seeing the very little of service I have seen, to waite the issue of that period rather than to hasten with too great precipitation from the army. Our beloved Children! I rejoice with you in their welfare. Dear Charles's Prayers, they must be heard. " Seigneur! tu as tiré ta gloire des Enfans " I remember to have caught my attention.

The welfare of the Dronfield cellar was still in his mind.

The Wine should certainly be kept constantly filled up. I hope it does not want much, but would advise purchasing, or borrowing, a Dozen or two of good Port rather than use what we have now in Bottles. Mr Smith will be likely to procure you some of the same with what I have drank with so much pleasure at his House. The Spring would be the best time for bottling one pipe and the other would improve in wood if kept for two years. I should not be in a hurry with it; and as this stock will enable us always to have wine six years in the cellar, I would not advise the parting with much. Don't engage yourself to part with more of it than you have already promised. The Duke you see is gone home; all is quietness here.

Five days later he added a postscript: " The Duke's family are ordered home. Every day brings us nearer together."

Poor William Harness could not foresee the terrible and fruitless winter campaign that for four long months was still to separate him from his family and his " dear cottage ".

Tiel, 18 December 1794

All here is quiet. I fancy we shall soon take up a fresh position, probably on the other side of the Rhine, as I find the Austrians are marching to relieve us and for the defence of the Waal. I am glad you have a map. The Austrians and Hanoverians occupy the Posts from Emmerich to the left of Nimmegan. The Brittish and Hessians extending to Bommel, the Picquets keeping up a constant chain along the bank of the River and furnishing Sentries at every fifty yards of this extensive line. You will see that the Duties are harrassing to our Troops at this severe season and that the Hospitals are consequently full. The Waal is very rapid, and the Enemy have neither boats nor Rafts to transport any force across it. At the same time every precaution is taken, so that their numbers can avail them not at all, and we have little chance of a visit. The strong little Town of Grave has been bombarded almost incessantly for the last three Weeks. It is commanded by a fine old Fellow of Eighty and upwards. The Town is surrounded and no succour can be administered but this excellent old

Fellow is determined (if his garrison will but stick by him, and this is not generally the faulty Post) to end his honorable life within the walls of his Government, or to submit to hunger alone. I understand he is provisioned for little more than a fortnight longer.

A few days later a party of the French did succeed in crossing the Waal, a minor exploit, so Major Harness supposed, that was likely to be made the most of by the press.

Tiel, 28 December 1794

The last week I past at Arnhem, spending the day in running along the banks of the Rhine in search of a Ferry to take me over it; none could I find, the masses of floating ice had carryed away every bridge. On Friday I past on the ice, and my Cart, for I had been for this ponderous Money, was drawn over likewise. We find to-day that a party of the French have crossed the Waal near Bommell in the same manner. The Bommelward has been ceded by the perfidious Dutch. Every Man in Holland is against the War. The want of confidence in allyed armies is always mischievous, but the present hatred of the Dutch is ruinous and would destroy better hopes than we can form. I believe it is determined to dislodge the small body of the Enemy whose temerity has brought them over the River. The report of this morning is that they have been driven back by the Hessians some credit is due to the account. I can easily suppose this event will give place to infinitely less probable reports in the English Papers; for we have seen that credulous Country put in alarm from accounts that deserve as little attention, by the flaming Editor of a News Paper, whose ignorance of the Geography of the Country, of position, and dispositions, can only be equalled by his absolute blindness of the force, even of ourselves. My Bessy will never let her judgement be drawn away by these hired pervertors of Truth. I have been led into this from your telling me you have the Courier, foreseeing that iniquitous paper will make a handle of the miserable people who in a fit of intoxication have past the Waal, without Guns and probably without provisions. What a diabolic Trade do these despicable wretches rest their subsistence upon!

An Officer of the 19th dined with us yesterday, he asked if I was not the Brother of the Physician General at Toulon, he discovered so strong a resemblance. He told me my brother's appointments there were immense, that he was in high health and very much liked.

The French were successfully dislodged on the following day and on 2 January 1795 Major Harness sent his wife an account of what he calls " the little affair "—which, however, it took six thousand men to accomplish.

Waardenberg, 2 January 1795

On the 29th of the last month I told you it was found necessary to dislodge a party of the Enemy from a position they had taken up on this side the Waal. On that Evening at 8 o'Clock fourteen Regiments of British including three of Cavalry marched from Tiel and the neighbourhood of it, through Buren for that purpose. We were joined by a Body of Hessians which augmented our force to about six thousand men. Between eight and nine in the Morning we found ourselves in the rear of the Village of Thiel, which the Enemy had nearly surrounded by a strong abbatis.[1] They had had intelligence of our designs and had been under arms from 4 o'Clock. They began the fire on our left, which was composed of six light Infantry Companies commanded by Lt-Colonel J. Champagné. Their first shot killed Major Murray who was at the head of the Lt Infantry Company of the 78th, three men fell by the same shot. We were formed immediately in the rear of the Village marching in open Column with our distances as exactly preserved as on the parade, when we received our orders to charge the Enemy, and drive them from the Village. The inter-sected ground, and ice in many places rotten, rendered this business somewhat difficult, but the spirit with which our good Fellows rushed on under a tolerably heavy fire soon surmounted every obstacle, and we were happy to see our object effected with very little loss. We took six Prisoners, and, what General Dundas' modesty will not let him tell the World, eleven Dutch Guns. We were under arms the next night, and the following

---

[1] Abatis—a defence constructed of felled trees, placed with their branches towards the enemy's line.

day marched into this Village. The General's thanks to this
little army on this occasion are very neatly expressed. Lord
Paget's determined coolness on this little affair, charging at the
Head of the Regiment, charmed every Soldier in it. The cold
is intense. I have been these two days at the Château de
Waardenberg, but am leaving it to be nearer the Regiment,
which is nearly half a mile in the Village. We are very comfortable.

The Waal was not held. A letter of 9 January, apparently
written from Eulemberg, reveals considerable puzzlement:

We left the banks of the Waal the day after my last and
marched to Buren, where we were two days, when we were
ordered to Schalkwyck on the other side the Rhine; but there
appearing to be some mistake in the General Orders we were
yesterday brought again over the Rhine and sent to this pretty
Town. There appears something that wants clearing up before
I can form a true judgement of the cause of so much motion.
The Enemy are driven from the Waal. The allied army is
instantly sent across the Rhine. The Enemy find no obstacle
to prevent them crossing the former River. They appear in
force on this side of it, possess themselves of the Towns and
villages on its banks and again our army are ordered from the
Rhine to dislodge them. If the idea is to maintain the Waal
why quit it? If it is expedient to evacuate it, why sacrifice so
many fine fellows in its defence? Nothing can be more comfortable than we are here and our sickness is getting under
considerably.

I have no doubt, my Bessy, that the Papers try to alarm you.
Conceive an army of 70,000 Men and the very few who meet
with a scratch. Colonel Buller and Colonel Hope were wounded
in the action yesterday but in an extent of line of thirty miles
five sixths of the army did not hear a shot. Indeed many
Regts have been out both campagnes without ever being
brought into action. At a distance it is supposed an army is in
continual danger, when, but for the parade, they would scarce
know they were not in England, and enjoy themselves shooting
and coursing and in some places hunting—for Sir Charles
Turner has his harriers with him. The Night Marches at this

season are certainly harassing, but what is wonderful the army was never so healthy as since it has been in motion.

Now began the slow, terrible withdrawal. The 80th were not with the main body of the army, but formed part of a separate detachment that was sent northwards under Lord Cathcart to West Friesland and Groningen. One object of this party was to investigate the sentiments of the Dutch people in those provinces. They did not discover much friendly feeling towards England. It was a frightful march. The cold was intense—it was the worst winter for a hundred years—the men were ill clothed and ill shod, the supply of rations inefficient, the enemy were pressing them closely. On 21 January Major Harness wrote from the town of Elburg on the Zuyder Zee.

The severity of the frost rendered our Posts on the Rhine totally untenable, from the length of our frontier and the numbers that opposed us in every quarter. We left Eulemberg very soon after my last which I hope you have received. I was obliged to send it by the Country Post. We were three days exposed without any shelter but what we could immediately construct with the willow bows and a little straw, lying on the Bank of the Rhine after having crossed that River on the Ice. From thence we fell back to Amersfoort, and two days ago to this town. The difficulties our poor people have had to contend with, by night marches, by cold, and by want of necessaries have been truly great, and have surpassed the strength of many a fine fellow, who sinking under them has been left frozen to death. Our stragglers are coming in every day. The miseries of the sick are too painful to write. Seven were found dead in one Waggon. The hardships of our brave Soldiery are really calamities. In reflecting on them, my affectionate wife will give too great a portion to her Husband. I am, my Bessy, little more than a Spectator of the wretchedness which surrounds me, possessing the means of defending myself, by additional cloathing and generous living, from the rigors of this climate at this season. Elberg you will see is on the Zuyder Zee, which is one immense sheet of ice. We expect to remain here for a few days and then continue our march for Emden, but with what intention I am not able to judge.

On the birth day[1] Lord Cathcart gave an elegant Dinner to the Field Officers. I had hoped to have partaken of the convivialities of our Village at this season, but fear it must be for a short time postponed. It is said transports are ordered round to Emden to convey the army to England and this is in some degree confirmed by a letter from a Gentleman at Portsmouth, the Brother of one of our Captains, who writes the same thing, and in addition informs us that Barracks are actually constructing all along the coasts and on the Isle of White.

The province of Utrecht has capitulated. The plunder of the rich Towns in Holland will furnish amply Booty to the devasting Enemy. I am sorry for the means this will furnish them for the prosecution of the War. Never was an event more disastrous to the allied Cause than the severity of this winter, which has given food and forage to the Enemy. It is supposed Lord Paget will go to England with his Brother.[2] It is wonderful to see with what ease he goes through the business. He has certainly a good deal of credit due to him. While the Enemy were moving in every direction, [and] large columns near, it was absolutely necessary to move in the night; but as the plunder of Holland is probably their main object, they have directed their march towards Rotterdam &c. We are here as much at our ease as in times of peace, collecting comforts for the men and repairing the injuries of our late hard marches, and preparing for leaving this Country.

A few days later Mrs Croke was writing to the worried young wife at Dronfield:

[1] Queen Charlotte's—18 January. She was actually born on 16 May 1744, but "As Her Majesty's birthday came within three weeks of that of the King, it was deemed advisable, for the benefit of trade, and public convenience, to celebrate the former on the 18th of January following, and ever after on the same day. That day was accordingly kept with great state and splendour at Court, the nobility and gentry vying with each other in richness of dress and grandeur of equipage." (J. Watkins, *Memoirs of Her Most Excellent Majesty Sophia Charlotte, Queen of Great Britain, from Authentic Documents*, 1819, p. 152.)

[2] "Lord Paget's Brother, who is our Minister at Berlin, is with us. He was on his way to England, but the communications by Helvoet being cut off, he has been by necessity compelled to take his quarters for a short time with us." (From another part of the same letter.)

Hampstead, 27 January 1795

You have well imagined, my Dearest Betty, the late anxiety I have felt on your and dear Mr Harness's account, for indeed I never suffer'd more than during the recent transactions in Holland. To hear that he was safe and well was joy indeed. When I last wrote to you how unexpected was this dreadful anxiety; but I think the next day brought the account of the perfidy and treachery of the French, and the severe setting in of the frost forwarded their diabolical purposes. How detestable are the Dutch for their conduct!

Turning to a more pleasant subject she went on to tell her country niece of the London fashions.

The hair is worn quite the same; the bonnets are very small and velvet most fashionable; Mrs P. intends buying herself one when she next goes to Town. I will get Swainson to copy it in paper or some way, and send it in the parcel. I don't think full muslin sleeves are now worn, but will enquire. Your sattin gown will only want a very short waist, plaited very far back; three broad tucks in it are enough—but more than four *must not be*. I dare say that you have strings on the sides of your stays to tie your coats up high to; or else the space from your gown through your upper coat will show itself and look ugly.

By 7 February the 80th had reached Hoogesondt, a village eight miles from the town of Groningen.

From Elburg I told you we expected to march for Embden. We left that Town soon after and marched for nine successive days till we reached this place. The object of this Column was to cover the retreat of the army, which from report had more to apprehend from the Dutch than from the French, sixty thousand men being said to be in arms at Groeningen to oppose our entrance into this Province. As we approached we every day found the validity of this report dwindle away, and that the National Cockade, which had been assumed by the Patriots,[1] again gave place to the Orange. Three Deputies

[1] The opponents of the Stadtholder Wilhem V. In 1785 he was driven by their action from the province of Holland and took refuge in Gelderland. He was restored in 1787.

from the City waited upon Lord Cathcart to represent the displeasure it might give to the Carmagnoles, to whom they had proposed terms of Peace, and whose constitution they had acknowledged, if they were to invite a Brittish army into the Town; but if he insisted upon entering it, the Gates should be thrown open and Quarters should be provided. Lord Cathcart led the Column to this place and Sutlers [1] and provisions are promised to be furnished us by the Magistrates. We have found the utmost hospitality wherever we have deserved it. Our men have suffered much from want of warmer cloathing during this month at this inclement season, but they had been trained to it by past exposure. For from 29th Decr, the day after they left Tiel, to 17th Jany includes a period of twenty days of as serious fatigue and hardship as most Campagnes can furnish. Seven nights we lay upon our arms, we had seven night marches, and the other six we were so near the Enemy as to sleep accoutred, ready to turn out at a minute's notice, and every morning under arms at five o'Clock and remained out till perfect daylight. When the universal intenseness of this winter is taken into the account, I think I may be justified in calling these twenty days of hard service.

We hear Transports are assembling to take us to England, but having had no news from thence since the 9th January, we must be in the dark as to the intentions concerning us. I regret the million endearing actions of our Charles! his present age is what calls out the fondness of a Father. Our Daughter is unknown to me. I have an acquaintance to make with my own Children.

This letter was finished on 16 February when the 80th had reached Leer in Hanover; and here at last the weary regiment found its long desired, long belated winter quarters.

Never did an army stand in greater need of rest, for our men are almost without Cloathes, for the last two or three days a large proportion were totally without Shoes marching bare foot. The Ice boats are well adapted for their purpose, taking out Passengers to Ships afloat. The thaw has continued

[1] Sutler. " One who follows an army or lives in a garrison town and sells provisions to the soldiers." (*Oxford English Dictionary*.)

for six days and in two or three more we hope the communication will be open.

Once in German territory they found at first a kindly and friendly population. At Leer they remained some six weeks. On 10 March 1795 the English cabinet decided on withdrawal from the Continent. On the 22nd began the march to Bremen, for it was there and not, as the earlier reports had said, at Emden that they were to embark for home. With the English at Leer was " a large body of Emigrant Corps ", and the bad behaviour of the Emigrant forces undermined to some extent the friendliness of the German inhabitants. At Leer William Harness was " living in a most comfortable house inhabited by an old lady, Madame Von Altena. She had a very fine Daughter here, but her fears of the Carmagnoles made her take flight, and she is gone to Bremen."

The weeks spent at Leer were not without their excitements. On 8 March Major Harness wrote of another " little affair " in which he bore himself with courage and distinction.

Lord Cathcart and his Corps have returned to this place after a most harassing march. Col. Champagné had the Command of the Light Companies and was nearly taken Prisoner. He was surrounded by the Enemy and saved himself by plunging into the water up to his neck. He had great difficulty to get across the inundation which was covered with rotten Ice, sometimes sliding for a few yards then dropping through. Lord Cathcart wrote to tell me his advanced Picquets had been driven in with some loss and that he should march with his whole force to the left during the night. The situation of this Town became of course very serious from the west side of the Ems, where the Enemy was in force, the Ice being passable every where on it for several miles. I employed six hundred men to cut the Ice and kept advanced Videttes on the other side. In this state a Flag of Truce appeared; on the Trumpet sounding all the Country people run away. Baron Dickenstein and myself past over, when the Carmagnole Officer told me three merchants from Hambro' wished to be passed over the Ice, and as they were neither French or Dutchmen he hoped their permission would be granted. There were reasons to suspect them and I refused them till the Commander in Chief's pleasure could be known. The same night two Dragoons from the Regt of Salm (an Emigrant Corps) deserted from a small fort we have at the Ferry and from the subsequent conduct of the Enemy we had reason to believe informed them of our weakness. Fortunately in the morning two Regimts marched into the Town with Col. McKenzie and Genl Dundas. A little after twelve o'Clock we heard a Gun, and very shortly after I received a report that the Enemy had driven our patrols across the river and were following them at full speed across the Ice, but that they had been stopped [by] a round of Grape. I hastened to Genl Dundas with the account, when we heard several Guns firing on both sides; he desired me to ride and see what was going on. I hastened to the ferry, where we had only a Subaltern and thirty Infantry, 15 Huzzars and 12 artillery; two of the latter were killed at their Gun just as I got up. Another 6 pounder we had in the fort I began to work, when one man was killed and another wounded at it, and the rest of the men were running from it. The Enemy were crossing on all sides; my thirty men I put under cover of the parapet and rode about encouraging them to the utmost of my power, begging them to spare their ammunition. I despatched a Huzzar to Gen. Dundas with a note requesting an immediate reinforcement. The Enemy still pressed on in considerable numbers and were within twenty yards of our parapet, huzzaing and making all sorts of shouting. Our Artillery we got again to their Guns, but our ammunition grew exceeding scarce, when the 33rd Regt appeared in sight. When they arrived we had not a single Cartridge left. Col. McKenzie came with them and desired I would remain with five Companies till more force arrived. It was with very sincere pleasure I saw the Enemy completely driven back again across the Ice. The consternation this little affair made in the Town will be better conceived when we recollect the distance Leer is from our late operations, and that the eldest Inhabitants had never heard the report of a Gun. I rode into the Town as soon as the business was over and the manner in which I was received testifyed their joy. I met Capt. Scott, the Genl's Aide de Camp, who congratulated me on the opportunity I had had of distinguishing myself. I have given you, my Bessy, a hasty, but plain, Sketch of all that past, but what I cannot tell the world. You see I make myself the principle figure in the piece and the world would call me Braggard; but it is to my wife, and the delight of rising in her estimation is too grateful to let pass this opportunity of declaring to her all the truth.

The Enemy have made no more attempts. The poor 80th lost all their Baggage which was cut off by a party of French Huzzars. I sent Carr fifty pounds two days before to distribute, the greatest part of which was taken. I hope to get it allowed. Five and twenty were made Prisoners. The present position is very strong from the Ice being too rotten to admit of passing over it, and while it continues no boats can cross, if the Enemy even had them, but they have not one.

A few days before these events, during the time of comparative quiet at Leer, Major Harness had written about a project for little Charles, which exemplifies the curious custom of the time.

1 March

Colonel C. has charged himself with getting *our Dear Charles an Ensigncy* and he will from it purchase him a Ltcy, when we will put him on Half Pay. I had half a mind to keep this a secret till you read it in the Gazette but as it is not likely to happen immediately I could not refrain mentioning his kindness to my own Bessy. Dear Charles's Lieutcy will be well worth the £150, the amount is about £40 per annum.

By 24 March the regiment was daily expecting an order to march to Bremen. Many of the sick were already on board the transports—" the Sentries from the other side say the French are quitting Holland, having drained it of their dirty Ducats ". Major Harness had had difficulty with his servants.

The Servant Dickenson, about whom you enquire, lost his road in a night march from Elburg. He followed the Greys, and I afterwards heard of him at Zwoll, enquiring for the Regt, but since that time not a word have I heard of him. He was a very sober, steady Man, and extremely willing. His having been bred a Taylor was against him as a Servant, but he improved daily and his desire to do well almost attoned for his want of knowledge at a time every exertion was called for. Poor Fellow, I had an excellent good opinion of him which he well deserved. I have been very unfortunate in Servants. I am at present almost without, altho nominally I have three, Two to take care of my horses and one myself; but they are people that require so much looking after that for one good one I might with great advantage exchange them all. The man I am obliged for his honesty to have with me is the best groom, so that my horses are sometimes neglected. I had a very fine one dyed on the march and was obliged to press another to get my Baggage forward.

On 4 April he wrote from Bremen full of happy anticipation.

We embark about forty miles from hence and I find the 80th is one of the ten Regiments that are destined for Portsmouth. My adored one, what transports will be ours! Your dear letter I received yesterday; that you are not in the best health grieves me, but I trust I shall find you well and plumped up. The very broken and interrupted rest, which added to our fatigues, and sometimes but moderate fare, you will perhaps, my Bessy, find has added a little to my age, although I believe I am fatter than when we parted. Bremen is a charming Town, but everything is so shamefully dear that I think you will excuse my executing your commission. I hope we shall meet by the 3rd May—another wedding day will be enchanting. The good old lady where I was billetted at Leer gave me a Ham when I came away, I had liked one I tasted at her house. I told her we would eat it on the 3rd of May and Drink her health. I left her a few bottles of Porter and she will remember us in one of them and wish prosperity to *my* Bessy, *our* Charles and *our* Jane. I hope to get leave the moment we land.

On the 3rd I dined with Prince Ernest of Mecklingburg, the Queen's Brother, his civility to the English is unbounded and it is partly from this cause I trace the very flattering attentions he was pleased to bestow upon me. General Duplatz had dined with me at Leer; he told Lord Cathcart I had been unusually civil to him. I found him at Oldenburg and he begged to

present me to the Prince which he did in the handsomest
manner. The Prince begged me to dine. We were a party of
eight, he placed me next him, and addressed himself almost
exclusively to me. After Coffee I took leave, he hoped I would
spend the following day with him, which not being able to do,
being sent forward hither on Brigade Business, he hoped I
would sometimes remember him when in England. How well
do Princes know how to attach, and what impression do we
receive from a few little attentions. Our vanity is so easily
flattered by them. I fear I have been a little tardy in giving
you information of the Poor Fellows you enquired after. It
often happens from the separation and the dispersion of the
Regiment that I can give no certain accounts of them. As
soon as we get to England and receive the Returns from the
Hospitals I will take care to get proper certificates of those of
my Recruits who have dyed to enable their unhappy Widows
to reap the benefit of the Subscription instituted for their
relief. I fear the catalogue will be a long one and am much
distressed at the fate of these fine fellows, who in some degree
attached themselves to me; but there has been no situation
where I could relieve that I have not tryed to do it.

The disastrous campaign was ended, and after an absence of
sixteen months William Harness was back with his family in
" the happy cottage ", as he called it—not exactly a conquering
hero, but a generous, humble-minded, patriotic Englishman
with a fine record of exacting duty bravely, conscientiously, and
capably performed. He arrived at Dronfield on the evening of
the wedding-day and it is to be hoped that he fulfilled the
expressed wish of his proud wife and children—" Pray bring
your Regimentals ".

5

French Adventure

FOR a few weeks after his return from Germany—in May, June, and July 1795—Major Harness was able to see something of his family. Then unexpectedly came orders to proceed abroad, and there followed another long parting.

In France the rising of the peasants of La Vendée, who had been joined in 1793 by the Royalist *Chouans* of Brittany, had proved a considerable embarrassment to the Republican Government. The *Chouans*, who took their name from a Breton word meaning " screech-owl " (an appropriate name because they were active mostly at night and used the hoot of an owl as a signal) were, at first, a wild and cruel horde composed mainly of smugglers and dealers in contraband. Under the Royalist noble, Charette de la Contrie, and other bold leaders they became a fearless army of many thousand daring adventurers. Charette, after taking part in the defence of the Tuileries, had retired quietly to the small Château of Fonteclause near the little town of Machecoul in Loire Inférieure. Here early in 1793 the peasants sought him out and begged him to lead them. Twice he refused. The third time they threatened his life if he would not accept the leadership. " Vous m'y forcez ", he said, " Je marche à votre tête "— and added that any disobedience would be severely punished.

Although at first an unwilling commander, Charette threw himself heart and soul into the cause. The spirit of his army changed. Their aims were not entirely unheroic, though it is to be doubted whether loyalty to the monarchy weighed so much with the peasant rank and file as annoyance at the new Government's interference with their settled habits: the enforcement of conscription, the suppression of their contraband trade, and the attacks on the priesthood; all these were bitterly resented.

In October 1793 Charette took possession of the Island of Noirmoutier, which enabled him to open communication with the English; but it was lost in the following January and there followed months of difficult campaigning during which Charette showed himself an admirable and resourceful partisan chief. In February 1795 a treaty was concluded and Charette made his entry into Nantes riding by the side of the Republican General Canclaux. His next entry into that city was to be very different. The Convention adopted a policy of conciliation and the famous Republican general, La Hoche, restored their cattle to those peasants who were willing to submit to the Government. But the armistice was not long lived. Royalist hopes had not entirely faded. An *émigré* expedition was equipped in England and in July Major Harness received his sailing orders and once more bade an indefinite farewell to his wife and children. They had joined him for a few weeks near Portsmouth, and he now left them with his brother's family at Wickham in Hampshire.

Some time before leaving England he had written, as he so often did, his thoughts and anxieties about the children's upbringing.

The dear children are losing their Derbyshire [accent?]. Don't, my dearest Bessy, permit them to touch a thing forbidden at table, or for a moment to do, or leave undone, but what and how you wish. I almost doubt whether that affectionate Duty to a mother which is lost at five years old is ever really recovered. Particularly with Boys, it should grow from their Infancy nor should they for an instant feel it is not as natural to obey the sollicitous care of a Mother as to walk or breathe. The habit will be formed before the rude age comes on, and you are saving a world of trouble.

How well Elizabeth carried out her children's training is evident in Charles's own letters.

On 27 July Captain Harness wrote to his wife's mother.

Convention off Plymouth

Mrs Bigg:

You have heard by my dearest Bessy of the temporary interruption of our Happiness thro' this sudden Embarkation,

The dear children amuse themselves admirably with their Cousins. Charles is quite a Jockey on the wooden Horse and John and William [1] drive Jane about with great glee in a little Phaeton they have.

We have with us six British Regiments, a great number of stores and Ordnance and several Hundreds of Emigrant nobility. They, poor people, are very sanguine, and probably, but for these unfavourable delays, not without good reason. As it is, I fear the happy season will be lost. I am told we are to be thrown into the strong town of Vannes while the Emigrants form a junction with Le Charette. I cannot but fear if we ever disembark on the French Coasts it will be but to embark again for the English, unless some very sudden and unforeseen event changes the face of things. I am in an excellent ship with a very pleasant party, and the Servant who was sent to me from the Continent I find a treasure: among his other talents he is a famous cook; in short my situation is as good as a transport can be. My health is very good, and but for the regrets at being separated from a most tenderly beloved wife I ought to be happy; and the consoling idea that I am performing my Duty to my Family and rendering our future situation easier ever affords me the most lively gratification.

The treasure of a servant was Zamor, of whom we hear frequently in later letters. He brought with him from his former employer a charming and pathetic letter [2] as an introduction to his new master.

Dipoltz, 26 avril 1795

Monsieur le major

Cette lettre sera vous presentée par le nommé Zamor qui va partir pour Portsmouth, avec le désir de faire tous ce qui dépendra de lui pour vous contenter. naturellement timide il demande à être conduit avec douceur. quant à la fidelité, j'en reponds comme de moi même & j'éspère que si j'ai jamais le plaisir de vous rencontrer, vous ne me ferez aucun reproche.

---

[1] Afterwards the Rev. William Harness, first Vicar of All Saints, Ennismore Gardens, the friend of Mrs Siddons, Byron, Miss Mitford, and many other well-known writers and actors. See my *Miss Mitford and Mr Harness*, 1955. *C.M.D.-J.*

[2] For translation see p 203.

c'est d'après cette assurance que je prens la liberté de vous le recommander, comme un Enfant que j'ai élevé depuis l'age de neuf ans, & au quel je suis fort attaché. sans les malheurs qui ont déchiré ma trop malheureuse patrie, je ne m'en serois jamais séparé. la paix va se faire, nous en serons bani pour toujours & je serai peut être trop content de pouvoir moi même trouver une place qui convienne un peu mieux à mon gout, que le métier que je suis obligé de faire pour procurer du pain à des êtres infortuné, *sans l'avoir merité*. Je ne dis pas même que plus tard je ne vous importune pour me recommander auprès de vos amis. destiné a servir dans l'artillerie, je sais les mathématiques & la Geographie, la fortification & je me chargerois volontiers de l'Education d'un ou deux Enfants, aux quels je pourrois en même tems montrer le françois—je dois ici, monsieur, demander Votre indulgence pour vous avoir parlé de moi, lorsque je n'avois à traiter qu'un sujet qui n'y avoit aucun rapport, & j'en reprens le fil pour vous prier que si, par des circonstances imprévus, vous ne pouviez garder Zamor comme votre domestique, vous ayez la bonté de le recommander à vos connaissances pour lui procurer une place. je ne vous parlerai point de ses gages: 30 guinées pour nourriture, Blanchissage & entretien sont un peu modiques, mais je ne doute point que lorsque vous le trouverez attentif à votre service, vous ne lui en donniez de suffisants pour qu'il soit dans une honnête aisance.

j'ai l'honneur d'être avec toute la consideration possible,

Monsieur le Major,
Votre très humble
serviteur P. REGNIER

A few days before Zamor's arrival William had written to his wife:

Cowes Roads, 20 July 1795

My dearest Bessy

The wind is fair, and the signal is just made for sailing. How auspicious, my only wife; I embark on the birthday of our Jane and sail on that of my Bessy! The weather is beautiful and all bears the fairest looks. Everybody in the Fleet are busy. The Bands are playing on all sides, and in every countenance is happiness and content. A short period will, I hope, render me both in the arms of my beloved Bessy. I shall drink your health. We have a very sober set on board.

As so often happened, contrary weather endangered the success of this not very hopeful expedition.

Convention off Plymouth, 27 July 1795

Again, my beloved Bessy, we are the play of this unfortunate wind and are obliged to put into Cawsand Bay. How uncertain are all operations which depend upon this fickle climate! Our Officers are gone on Shore to get provisions, which this lengthened out little voyage has made necessary. To-morrow it will be a fortnight that our people have been on board this Vessel; when we embarked we believed three or four days would have taken us to our destination. It is now said that we are to garrison the Strong Town of Vannes, while the Emigrants again reembark to join La Charette, who is said to be in very great force; but whatever is our object this delay must be extremely unfavourable to its success.

And still the unfavourable wind continued to hamper proceedings:

Plymouth Sound, 31 July, 1795

This contrary wind has so long detained us here, my dearest Bessy, that our expedition becomes every hour more doubtful. The ill-success of the poor Emigrants, and the perfidy of the Prisoners,[1] so impolitickly mixed with them, and the frightful loss of stores to the value of a million sterling weigh powerful on the judgement in making up an opinion on this subject.

The letter concludes:

Our expedition, my Bessy, is at an end. We have it announced, but we know not whether we are to return to Portsmouth or to remain here; in a few days I shall see you. How prophetick have been my fears! I foresaw the strange mis-

---

[1] Over 1600 French prisoners-of-war had been released to take part in these ill-fated expeditions. Many of them deserted to the Republicans.

conduct of emptying Gaols for Royalists, indeed the Prisoners declared publicly their intention. This failure will make a considerable noise in Town and blame will attach.

It had looked like the final crushing of Royalist aspirations when, on 20 July La Hoche had wiped out an *émigré* force. Another attempt, however, was yet to be made and William Harness was in it. In this fresh expedition the French emigrants, who accompanied the English force, had with them an exalted companion. The exiled Comte de Provence, brother of the ill-fated Louis XVI, had, on the supposed death of his nephew, taken the title of Louis XVIII. His brother, the Comte d'Artois (afterwards Charles X) with a considerable staff, formed part of this latest expedition. On 13 September the parties had reached Quiberon Bay and William Harness wrote:

After a good deal of unfavourable wind and weathering a slight gale, we arrived safe here yesterday morning. We are in this Bay, at an extremity of it, and have no communication with any part of the Country immediately about us but a small Island that is not able to furnish us with water. Sir John [Warren] shewed me two Broomsticks armed with a ruff piece of iron, which composed the arms of the Royalists and with which they put to the rout ten regular Battalions of the republican troops. He has sent them arms which they have received, and with such joy, that they kissed them while they threw down their miserable pikes. It is supposed that we shall remain in this neighbourhood ready to succour them. Monsr D'Artois dined yesterday with Sir John and was received with regal Honors. I don't hear of any particular losses sustained in the last gale. We heard that two ships were obliged to put back to England. Our Fleet is very considerable consisting of a hundred and thirty sail.

Quiberon, 23 September 1795
On the 17th we sailed for Noirmoutier but, the wind setting against us, we were obliged to return hither after four days struggle in which we did not advance more than ten miles. Several of the Ships are in want of water and most of those

with Horses on board are not only without it, but in total want of forage. We have sent our boats on shore at a small Island and dug two wells, which will prove a supply should we stand in need of them. I should not be much surprised at our return to England without making any attempt, anxious as I dare say everybody in England are to hear that the Emigrants are well off our hands. The Coasts are all along peopled with large Towns and the length of time that has been given to the Enemy to fill them with Troops, as well as with every article of military stores, renders the improbability of this small force attaining its object but daily the more impracticable. We are very fortunately remarkably well, not having a sick man on board. I fancy we are considerably warmer than in Hampshire, and having so many men on board for so long a time, to prevent the crowd of them below, I have prevailed upon the Captain to spread awnings over the Decks, under which two thirds of our people sleep while at anchor.

The Ile de Yeu (sometimes called Ile Dieu) is a rocky islet of eight and a half square miles lying some twenty miles off the coast of La Vendée. (It gained some notoriety in recent years as the place of confinement of Marshal Pétain.) Here, after the Royalist defeat, a large number of refugees from the mainland had been landed by Sir John Warren. Their lot was not enviable, but they did at least escape the butchery that befell many of their comrades at the hands of the victors. On 3 October William Harness wrote to his wife from this desolate spot.

A few days after my last we sailed from Quiberon for Noirmoutier with the intention of attacking it, but the night on which the attack was to have been made Sir John Warren received letters from Charette to say a hundred and twenty pieces of cannon were mounted on the Island, that it was defended by a powerful Garrison, and that the conquest could be but of little use to him as he would have three forts to pass before he could communicate with us and that each of them had been reinforced. It was therefore determined to send the twelfth and us to take possession of this miserable Island,[1]

[1] The " miserable island " has now become a pleasant holiday resort

where we found about a hundred Republican troops without any means of defence. A Flag summoned the Island in the name of Louis 18th; they answered they were ready to cede it to the British but would not acknowledge Louis 18th.[1] We marched into camp where we remain, and Monsr and the Emigrants with the other two Regiments came to us and landed yesterday. I fear we have a miserable prospective of working a Revolution. I fear too we are much deceived as to the Opinions of the People, and that we shall find ourselves dreadfully deluded if we are led into hopes of drawing much assistance from Charette. His army is formidable but from their position, and not of a nature to march out in quest of conquests. It is composed of the peasants who assemble for a few days at the ringing of the bells, and disperse again among their bogs to their Families.[2] We have regular correspondence with him, and I doubt not shall be able to get rid of our immense stores and as much money as we please to send, in short of everything that has a value; but the time of effectual operation is lost. The army of the Pyrenees covers the coasts and are not I should suppose a little pleased to see us shutting up our force and confining their Enemies the Emigrants on this barren Island. The Inhabitants of it are said in peace to amount to nearly two thousand men, but the men have been forced to serve in their Navy, and we find scarcely anything but women and children. A little corn is grown, and I am told there are about eighty head of horned cattle on the Island and about four times that number of sheep, but very small, as you will conceive when I tell you five are bought for a guinea. The occupation is fishing, we hear the fish is excellent, but for almost everything else I find they send to the Continent. An Inhabitant, quite à la Française, informed me they were supplyed from thence with every article down to a Match to light their Candles. England will of course supply us—as long as it is judged expedient to keep us here. Monsr is setting out in a great way, having demanded a hundred Rooms for himself and suite. I am afraid he will be very unpopular with the

[1] In a letter to Mrs Bigg, Major Harness adds that " the Mayor, who is their Governor, refused to acknowledge him ".

[2] One is forcibly reminded of the heroic and ill-used Mihailovich and his Chetniks.

British. The officers' horses are ordered to be kept in camp as the whole stabling is declared insufficient for him. There are an abundance of Hares and Partridge but shooting is forbidden. Fortunately, having had two or three days to look about us, we have been able to stock ourselves with whatever we shall want till supplys from England arrive.

Isle Dieu, 14 October 1795

Days and weeks roll on, my beloved Bessy, without giving us one word from England. General Doyle has not had the scratch of a pen since he left it. When will the joy be given me of hearing from you. We are living in so regular a way on this little Island, one day seems so much like another that a sheet of paper would give the whole history of us since our landing on it. We are all in good health. We look out with anxiety for provisions from England. This small encompassed spot is nearly exhausted. The Emigrants brought nothing from England. Monsieur and Eighteen of his Suit dine every day with General Doyle. He is extremely gay, and has spirits that no trick of fortune can effect. The little French I speak caused him to address himself yesterday at the General's table a good deal to me. The Duke de Bourbon has left us. Monsieur and he are not the best Friends. Some years ago they had an affair of honor.[1] Monsr had taken too great pains to insinuate himself into the good opinion of Madame de Bourbon. The Duke de Chatillon is here, he has dined, supped and breakfasted with me. He is sorry he did not know you at Hampstead. A French Frigate has just passed through our harbour. She was thought to be English, when she had gotten to a small distance she hoisted her French colours. Sir John Warren and another Frigate are gone after her, but I fear she is too far for them to come up with her. The wind here is very squally, particularly they say at this season. We have such gusts of wind and violent showers that we can scarcely get our marquees to stand, the poor fellows' tents are constantly blown up.

---

[1] " Il dut un jour en 1778 accepter une rencontre avec le Duc de Bourbon, dont la femme avait été l'object de son impertinence au bal de l'Opéra. Les deux princes se battèrent, ou firent semblant, car ils n'avaient ni l'un ni l'autre l'humeur fort belliqueuse." (A. Debidour in *La Grande Encyclopédie*.)

By 25 October this dreary life was still unrelieved by the longed for news of the loved ones at home.

Again, my dearest, has the Packet sailed without our letters. We have not had a word from England. We yesterday marched from camp into cantonments. The wind and rain have rendered it quite necessary, but the difficulty was to find houses. We are in two miserable villages. The Houses are but of one room with two doors, which are opposite to each other, one serving for a window or a door as the wind blows. I have fortunately a window in mine. The wretched Inhabitants are put pell mell into a few houses that are allotted them, and the soldiers take possession of the rest. The distress of these poor people, carrying their beds about, is painful to witness. They are civility itself but this in no way diminishes the sufferings they undergo from a brutal Soldiery, who take advantage of their consternation to plunder them; but I am happy to see every precautionary means taken to prevent as well as the strongest measures to punish these disorders.

What, my Bessy, can be the cause of no vessell arriving from England? Are we forgotten? If we have not soon supplys we must get into our ships and return to England. This begins to be seriously spoken of.

It is reported that Commissioners for peace are in London. Again that Sixty thousand of the army in Normandy have deserted, that the Members of the Convention are cutting each other's throats. We are amused with a thousand extravagances as is ever the case with people who are cut off from information. Sir John Warren gets letters from General George the Chief of the Chouans. He gives him his wishes, I believe, for realities.

Isle Dieu, 6 November 1795

Monsieur de Chatillon has just left me. He is in low spirits on the prospect of a peace. I was surprised at those of Monsieur who I met yesterday at General Doyle's. His are unchanged but he tells me he sometimes sees him in private when he is in real depression, but that the moment a person enters to whom he is not intimately known, he puts on the shew of his natural character.

If we return soon to England I will hasten to meet you at

Dronfield, and should a peace be made I hope we shall remain there some time. I have an Island cow. We must contrive a place for it.

So the dismal weeks dragged on; and supplies were running very low. On 2 November Major Harness had written:

We begin to be in serious want of provisions. You know we have the ship rations for a considerable time. We have flour, but wine, tea, sugar and a thousand little articles that make up subsistance the whole Island is in want of. Col. Champagné and I by good fortune and management are not in the distress we see our neighbours, but a short time will leave us too destitute of these comforts—unless some supplys arrive. They cannot be long. To what are we to attribute this indifference about us? As to everything that concerns our security we have nothing to apprehend, but for the rest another fortnight will reduce us to an uncomfortable situation.

Four days later a Packet arrived, so probably the " uncomfortable situation " was alleviated. With the departure of Monsieur later in November (the exact date of the letter is missing) came the beginning of the end of this strange little adventure.

Monsieur you know has left us. A more affecting public scene I never experienced. He is ordered to Spithead where a ship is to be provided for him to take him whithersoever he pleases. Poor fallen Greatness! or rather fallen state! for from his greatness he will never fall! To how few corners of the Globe can he direct his course. His manners are extremely elegant. His leave on the beach, I know not why, drew tears from many *English*, who have been lately in the habit of meeting him at table. The adieu he gave to every Body was so varied and so feeling, at the time he seemed to feel so little for his individual state, that it will be very long remembered by all. The Corps of Cadres, the Prince de Leon's, but commanded here by his relation, the Duke of Chatillon, is gone to Jersey. He came to take leave of me, asked if you were in town, and promised to call on you. You will see that all hopes of achievement in this quarter leave us with these Corps. The Corps of Cadres is composed of Gentlemen who were to have been Officers had we succeeded. The Chouans are however in greater force than ever and are this day to make a grand attack to endeavor to get possession of the coast. Sir John Warren and his Squadron are gone to Quiberon with Stores. It is said the Republican force had been drawn off in that quarter against Charette. We have no news of our return.

At last, on 4 December, there was more definite news of the return to England. It was a joyful husband who wrote that

A cutter will sail immediately and I am very anxious to tell you by it that the Twelfth Regiment have this morning embarked for England, that we are all coming home. General Needham has just sent to ask Col. Champagné, Major Ford and myself to accompany him on board the Theseus. We expect to embark about Monday or Tuesday and shall probably sail in about ten days after, or less. I am wild with the idea of meeting my adored wife.

On 17 December he wrote from the *Prince of Wales* in Quiberon Bay:

The last division of the army from Isle Dieu is in sight. I sailed as I told you in my last in the Theseus from Isle Dieu, but Admiral Harvey taking one half the Regiment in this ship I have been sent with them. His civilities are very flattering, he has done me the Honor to give me the half of his Cabin and his Table. It is a week that I have been embarked— where, my beloved, shall we meet? Will it be at Wickham or at Aylesbury? It is so long since I heard from you that I scarce know where to direct this letter.

The admiral was civil, the company was pleasant, William Harness was embarked for home, but again there is the same story of unkind winds. On 26 December the *Prince of Wales* was still in Quiberon Bay.

The Galatea, my dearest Bessy, is getting under way. I have one instant to tell you the anxiety with which we are detained in this Bay by contrary winds. The Admiral is very careful of his Convoy, and with so great a charge cannot sail but with moderate weather. My Bessy can only judge of what I feel. Little did I expect the possibility of remaining so long here. We every hour expect the change of this horrid Wind.

After this there is a gap in the series of letters, so we may assume that the " horrid Wind " did change at last and that Major Harness was able to sail for home. The expedition, as was only to be expected, had been a failure, but the husband and father was restored to the bosom of his family. Presumably he brought his island cow with him. Until April 1796 he remained in England.

Sir John Fortescue wrote forcibly of this reckless and ill-fated venture:

I incline to the opinion that this [expedition] to the Isle d'Yeu was the most disgraceful, in point of negligence and reck-lessness, that was ever thrust by a British Minister upon a British General. It is perfectly plain that no pains whatever were taken to obtain accurate information ... before the force was despatched to sea, and that the Ministers had really not the vaguest notion of what they really meant it to accomplish. If they intended it to land and act with the Vendeans, it was too weak to be of the slightest value. If they designed it, as they professed, to seize and guard some island on the French coast, as a depot from which to furnish the Vendeans with supplies and stores, then it should have been fully equipped with victuals for several months and with the means of erecting shelter; and the cavalry, with its two thousand horses, should have been left at home. But to consign three thousand infantry and two thousand cavalry, without any reserves of food or forage, in the month of September to a barren rock in the Atlantic, where there was no safe landing-place and conse-quently no assured communication with the outer world—this was something more than a blunder! it was a crime. . . . So great were the risks of the voyage that, though the garrison would have given almost any price for soap and candles, no adventurer would hazard the shipment of a cargo to the island.[1]

[1] *A History of the British Army*, Vol. 4, *1789-1801*, 1906, Bk. XII, p. 422.

The return of Monsieur to England, without even attempting a landing in France, was the death-blow to Charette's hopes. But would such a landing ever have been possible or effective? Whether through pride or defiance, the gallant Royalist leader refused a free passage to England. In the last weeks of his resistance he led a hunted life with only thirty-two of his followers still round him, himself wounded and carried on the shoulders of his men. He was taken on 23 March 1796 and shot at Nantes a few days later.

What manner of man was this Monsieur, who was later to succeed his two brothers as King Charles X? It is clear from Major Harness's letters that he possessed graciousness of manner and royal charm. D'Artois had been a pleasing, attractive boy, but his upbringing in a corrupt court brought out the less aimable sides of his character. He was at once a bigot and a libertine. Unlike his brother, the Comte de Provence (Louis XVIII), he had not the common sense, when he came to the throne, to act the part of a constitutional monarch. He declared that he would rather hew wood than " be a king under the conditions of the King of England ". With Queen Marie Antoinette he had been the soul of the counter-revolutionary coterie. After the fall of the Bastille he was a leader of the stream of emigrants, and took upon himself the task of rousing the sovereigns of Europe against his country. When, in 1791, Louis XVI appealed to his brothers to recognize the Constitution they both replied—" avec‘impudence " says a French writer—that they could not obey a captive sovereign.

D'Artois was not the bold, princely leader whom Charette awaited. " Sire ", wrote that disappointed man to Louis XVIII, " la lâcheté de votre Frère a tout perdu; il ne me reste plus qu'à me faire tuer inutilement pour Votre Majesté." Yet had Monsieur been cast in more heroic mould, would it have made any difference in the final result of the rising?

6

Sojourn at the Cape

THE LONG arm of Napoleon was reaching out towards India, and in 1796 came the longest parting of William Harness and his wife. It was a hard time for him to leave her, for Elizabeth was expecting her third child. On 9 April the 80th embarked at Gosport in an Indiaman—the *Lion*. All was " hurry and confusion ", and the Major himself was in a state of acute depression and anxiety. He had had two pieces of news from the faithful " Aunty Croke "—the death of Elizabeth's mother and, the next day, a fortnight before she was expected, the birth of delicate little Jemima Elizabeth—" little Bessy " as her father called her.

The little girl's first name did not please her parents. It was given at the request of Miss Alethea Stephens, the great-aunt at Bath, a lady, as we know, full of kindness but of whom her great-niece stood somewhat in awe. " My brother," Miss Stephens had written, " desires you should consider him as offering his Name the next occasion, whether for Masculine or Feminine, as James does not sound amiss converted into *Jemima*, which will be a new name in the Family if you do not *mislike* it." Elizabeth did mislike it, but she dutifully acquiesced. " We must not affront him, but I shall not like the name of Jemima."

By the time his second daughter was born the regiment was on the march and, though still in England, it was impossible for Major Harness to visit his wife and baby. He wrote to Mrs Croke:

Your kindness will do much to re-establish my Bessy. Poor Infant, I hope it is better. You see by the incoherence of this paper the but too plain traces of a mind not at ease. A little quiet will compose, and I shall again feel a solid satisfaction in undergoing the Duties of my Profession for the prosperity of my beloved Home.

Can we of the present day, living in our more convenient, if not altogether happier, circumstances, envisage at all what such a separation meant? There were the far greater hazards of travel, the uncertainty of future plans and, above all, the difficulties of communication—no telegrams or air mail, and often eleven months or more before a letter reached the army in the East (at Alexandria on 10 January 1802 William Harness received a letter from his wife written on 15 November 1800). With what anxiety would the soldier imagine the disasters that might have overtaken his loved ones in those long-drawn months—illness, bereavement, money troubles. For a long period William was deeply worried by the news of a considerable financial difficulty, in which his Bessy was involved through no fault of her own. This " strange scrape ", eleven months old when her husband first heard of it, was due to the failure of a trusted friend and agent. Help was forthcoming from two of Elizabeth's devoted aunts. " My good Aunt Croke supplies me; as long as she has it I shall not want, but you know her income is not large." Another aunt, Miss Bigg of Aylesbury, also helped her niece out of her small income; and her brother-in-law, John Harness, " Physician to His Brittanic Majesty's Fleet ", wrote from H.M.S. *Saturn* off Lisbon, offering to advance her a sum of £150 to £200. But all this was ancient history before the worried husband was able to make any arrangements to ease the situation.

A sorrow more poignant than any was the separation from the children, who were growing up without knowing their father; the missing of those precious nursery years without even the small consolation of photographs to record their appearance and progress or lively snapshots of everyday family doings at home. Every letter from William Harness bears witness to his painful longing for news of the little details of life in the beloved home at Dronfield.

The first destination of the regiment in its passage to India was Capetown. Since our former allies, the Dutch, had concluded " an offensive and defensive alliance " with the French they were now considered as enemies. In the previous year the

British had therefore seized both the Cape and Ceylon as being important strategic points on the route to India. By 12 April 1796, when the *Lion*, with the 80th Regiment on board, had reached St Helen's in the Isle of Wight, William Harness was more composed: " I find, my Bessy, my spirits improve. The Wind is delightful, the weather fine and we sail under the fairest prospects." There is a gap now in the letters, for some were lost. " I read some time ago ", wrote Elizabeth several months later, " that the *Friendship* was taken and the letters thrown overboard. You confirm what I then conjectured that by that ship you gave me an account of your voyage."

The next letter is dated 2 August, by which date the ship had reached the Cape after a voyage that had been indirect and unusually slow. Major Harness speaks here of other letters " giving an account of our passage, tedious as it has been. We expected ", he says, " to put into St Salvador or Rio Janeiro, near to both of which places we were driven. You will see in your Map those places within the Tropics in South America. Few of the Captains of Indiamen have before experienced so long a passage hither." He goes on to voice his dismay at South African prices.

The Impositions here are frightful, but mostly from our own Country Men. Finding the Garrison in want they are all extortioners. Porter a Guinea the Dozen. Whatever is the produce of this Colony is cheap, which fortunately comprehends every article of the first wants; but whatever is imported from Europe or Asia is mounted to a price beyond all bounds. A coat, Zamor tells me, would cost him ten Guineas. This rapacity will destroy itself, for as soon as it is understood that there is a market the English merchants will send out ventures. The Climate, the General tells me, is the finest in the world and even in December and January there is an elasticity in the air that renders the heat very supportable.

On 20 August there was a hurried note from Soldanha Bay, where important events had taken place. General Craig and Admiral Sir George Elphinstone, who had been so largely instrumental in the capture of the Colony, were still on the spot.

I have one single moment to tell you that nine Dutch Ships of War have just fallen into the hands of Sir George Elphinstone and General Craig. They have been ten days in this Bay. The Admiral appeared at the mouth of the Bay at the instant General Craig shewed himself on the heights with twenty-five hundred men. The March has been attended with difficulties which will be detailed, I presume, by the General. The distance about 90 miles from the Cape Town. We are all perfectly well. I write from a crowded Soldiers' tent. You will see particulars in the Admiral's and General's letters. Nothing could have been more compleat. If we share prize money with the navy mine will be considerable, at the least five hundred pounds.

The commander of the Dutch fleet had probably counted upon a rising of the Dutch in the Colony. But General Craig acted promptly and with his 2500 men was there in time after a gruelling nine days march.[1] No rising took place.

A note written on 1 September, enclosing a lock of her husband's hair, told Elizabeth that he was returned to Cape Town " in perfect health but have not had off my Cloaths for three weeks ". After an expedition that " has been toilsome but happy, you will be delighted ", he says, " with our captures. The Fleet are all lying in the harbour here and they are landing the Prisoners." A long letter was promised and six days later William Harness found time to write much more fully of his impressions of the country. During several weeks his time was much occupied by a " frightful General Court Martial "—certainly a trying experience to a kindly-hearted man.

Good Hope, 2 August 1796
There are two or three Officers of the 28th Dragoons to be brought before us. We yesterday tryed a poor fellow for

---

[1] Fortescue thus describes this journey: " This was the first real march ever made by British troops in South Africa, a dreary tramp of ninety miles through so barren a country that but five houses were seen in the whole of it. The burghers with surprising readiness helped Craig to impress waggons and cattle, as well as horses and saddles for the cavalry; but even so, the subsistence of the force was with difficulty provided for. The men suffered every privation except that of meat, and the column took nine days to reach Soldanha Bay." *History of the British Army*, Vol. 4, *1789-1801*, 1906, Book XII, p. 508.

Murder. He had returned a Blow given in a hasty moment by his comrade and fractured his Skull. They had lived as brothers and come from the same place.

Among those brought before a Court Martial in Cape Town was young James, the former servant of Major Harness, who after being treated with much kindness and forbearance had finally been dismissed for dishonesty, but upon whom his late master still kept a fatherly eye.

You will be shocked to hear James is under the sentence of a General Court Martial for breaking open a house. The sentence is not yet made public but the evidence was so black against him, that I fear it is death.[1] He sent to me to give him a Character. It is given upon oath, but had it been without that solemnity I could not have broken my word by adducing anything in his favor. I am very much concerned for him, and still more for his family, should the unhappy account reach their ears.

Here are William Harness's impressions of the march to Soldanah:

Good Hope, 6 September 1796

I will take the leisure I can steal from this frightful General Court Martial, which is resumed, to write to you. Our Prizes I find I underrated, as you will have seen by the gazette Accounte. They are not only very advantageous to the Nation, but particularly likely to turn out so to the Captors, should not so solid a good escape from our hands into those of the Gentlemen at Westminster Hall. I find Sir George Elphinstone yesterday waited on General Craig in the name of the Navy to disavow any claim or title the army might make to a Share in the Prizes, and to inform us that their agent would be instructed to resist any claims we might set up in a Court of Law. Foreseeing a possibility of a step of this kind on the part of the Navy, the General took the precaution the morning of the Capture to call the Field Officers of the Army together to

---

[1] We hear in a later letter that the errant James escaped with 300 lashes and was returned to his regiment.

appoint an Agent, to send him letters of Attorney, to impower him to draw seven Hundred Pounds on our Accounts for the purpose of maintaining the Suit, and to instruct him to stop the Contemnation of the Ships for the Navy till our Claims were determined. In addition he wrote a Memorial to the King representing in the strongest terms our title and requesting his Majesty and Council would be pleased to decide between us and spare the vexation, delay and expence of a Decision by the Courts at Law. Should we succeed, and no one here entertains a doubt on the Subject, my share is guessed at a Sum between £1000 and £1500. The 33rd Regiment which was going out to India the General has detained here, on the information of the Dutch Fleet that they were to have been joined by a French Fleet, whose object was nothing less than the possession of this valuable Colony. The whole of Sir George's Fleet is riding in this Bay. A great number of Prisoners have entered and are distributed through the Fleet. Several Hundreds have engaged into the East India Service, so that the acquisition of strength is great with respect to men, and Seamen as well as Ships.

I have told you nothing of our March or the Country we past through, which is almost universally wild, bold and in general uncultivated. Mountains on whose summits rest Clouds that the eye cannot pierce; Houses scattered many miles asunder, within large quadrangles with high walls, within which their immense droves of cattle are sheltered at night, but which are squandered over the Vallies by day. The cultivated spots bear everything that is committed to them and in abundance. I see the richest crops of grain spring out of sands I can scarce walk through. We had several Ostriches Eggs brought to us and found them of an excellent flavour. The Gentlemen amused themselves with shooting Deer, Hares and Birds of various kinds. I went out one day but was unsuccessful, however was amused seeing De Lancey gallop at full speed five or six miles after an Ostridge which run much at its ease before him. Our Marches were very long.

Colonels Champagné and Ramsey, till he was obliged to return very ill, Carr and myself occupyd a soldiers tent. As we had no beds I took the precaution to take with me a Zebra's Skin, which defended me from the wet ground, and a Blanket was our covering, our small portmantuas served for pillows.

At Groen Cloft we got into a small hut from which its having in it two Hornet's nests (which we found troublesome neighbours) Ramsey christened Hornet Hall. Champagné wrote a note to the General, who fortunately came up in the nick of time, to request a Bottle of wine if he wished to spare the lives of three or four of his Friends in the miserable hut. He sent us a Bottle of rum with a caution to use it sparingly as he had but very little. The treat gave a *Cream* to our features. We borrowed the Soldiers Camp Kettles to dress our Dinners, fortunately Carr had his Canteens from on board; but to see the shifts our friends were put to for plates, knives, Forks and Spoons and their ingenuity in supplying these wants would amuse. Tomahaks cut the meat into pieces, sea Shells made admirable Spoons, a stick cut picked a fork, and the shell of the Land Tortoise which were found in profusion in different sizes served a variety of purposes.

The Heaths were beautiful to a degree, as well as many of the flowers; the Geraniums of several kinds we were obliged to clear away to pitch our tents. I have been very idle, not to read botany, or to learn how to select from these wild and vast vegitable Kingdoms. I yesterday dined with General Doyle on a Porcupine. We have here a king or chief of the Caffres and his wife, a very strong, active and dextrous animal. They are almost naked. They dance and beg about the streets. An artist is taking his picture, the resemblance is a good one, it will probably find its way into print in England. An expedition moves to-morrow into the interior. It is represented that conventions are held, and that they have attempted to cut off our supplys. Their numbers have been considered so contemptible that the General has left them to themselves till this imprudence of theirs. He now sends Major King with the Light Infantry, Hottentot Corps, and two Hundred Dragoons, and should not the unhappy people return to their Houses and possessions he has orders to burn them. I feel for these people without a military force, without support or means, and whose only crime is attachment to the Government they have been born and nourished under. It requires time to conciliate the minds and turn the habits of men unused to courts.

The Climate is now moderate, the mornings are very warm but we have a breeze springs up generally in the middle of the day. After the Court Martial, which confines me till 3 o'Clock, I take exercise on horse back till five. The Horses are light, of the Spanish kind, very pretty and fleet. I have two very good ones.

8 September

I am told some of the Principle Inhabitants are to be brought before our Court Martial. They had taken the oath of allegiance, and were discovered giving intelligence to the Dutch Admiral. I fear at the Bottom they do not like us. The Captain of the Tromp has a wife and family here. I had the command of the Guards and marched the Prisoners through the Town to the Amsterdam Battery, where they are lodged. At every Door and Window you saw nothing but mournful Countenances and dejection. General St Leger we are told is coming out, and going on to India. There was a report of the 80th going on, but it is done away by the arrangement which is made with regard to troops at this station. General Craig tells me it is fixed that the Regiments are to be relieved here every five years and afterward go forward for another five years. Of necessity in time of war this plan will not unfrequently be broken in upon. Would to God, I could hold out any time fixed for seeing my beloved better Self.

In September Major Harness had news of his promotion to Lieutenant-Colonel.

22 September

My Promotion, my dearest wife, took place on our wedding day. How distinguished is that charming day. Had it appeared before I left England, I should have been tempted to have made an excuse to stay at home. But Heaven determines for us. I hope our sufferings will be rewarded. I expect at least a thousand pounds from our captures.

His wife is treated to some of the gossip of the regiment:

My Company I should wish the payment of to Harvey.[1] It would be two Shillings a day to him but his giddiness will not permit me. It would ruin him and the Company. What a

[1] A young officer, also from Dronfield, a protégé of William Harness.

97

pity that, with good dispositions and very good sense, much as I long to serve him, a certain desire of doing like the young men who have better means, (for that I take it is the Principal cause), deprives me of all power of doing it. He has lost the good wishes of Colonel Ramsey for life by amusing Captain De Lancey while on board *with his ideas* of the oddities of that excellent old Officer, not knowing the Colonel was in the Cabin and heard every word. I very seldom see Mrs Molony, when I do she always in the kindest manner enquires after you. He is a frightful man, and is not at all liked. I see him but on the parade, and speak distantly to him when off it should I meet him. Captain Rooke has taken the payment of his Company from him. In short I believe he is not honest. He absolutely stole a case of Spirits of mine on board. You see, my Bessy, it is to you only I can accuse a Gentleman of such a crime but the fact is but too certain. You will not let this circumstance escape your lips.

With the stocking of his own and his friends' cellars still in mind Colonel Harness set himself to procure some casks of the most famous wine of the country. " I will try to get a little Constantia to send Mr Smith ", he wrote on 22 September. " It is very scarce, but such friendship deserves every remembrance." A few days later he was successful.

Good Hope, 3 October 1796

I send two Casks of Constantia, one of white and one of Red, all the General's Secretary could procure for me, to Lord Harrington. He most particularly desired me to procure it for him, and I have been in great apprehension I should not succeed. I am on the look out for my own Bessy. It is more curious than really good, and very expensive. The Casks are very small and cost twenty pounds. It will perhaps surprize you to know I have tasted it but once since I have been here. It was at the General's table. It was produced for Colonel Aston and some of us who had never tasted it. You know it is to be purchased but of one man, who lives at Constantia, and he parts with his best but capriciously. He is suspected of being a little disaffected, in spite of the immense prices he gets for his wine.

By the time you receive this most probably England will be wrapt in snow, and we shall be panting for breath. Christmas you know is midsummer at the Cape. Like all other places in possession of the English, or where they much resort, this is becoming shamefully extravagant. Fowls have risen to three and sixpence a piece, Eggs Twopence, and every thing but bread almost in proportion. Our Soldiers get a pound and an half of meat and a pound of bread for two pence half penny; but perhaps the rapid and great advance of provisions may be owing to the increased demand by an increased population of at least fifteen thousand, including the Garrison and Fleet, and the difficulty of getting up the supplys from the interior parts of the Settlement. The Company's Gardens are now the place where every Body walk in the Evenings. The walks are avenues of very fine Oaks planted so thick as to be impervious to the rays of the Sun. The Ladies you would take to be English till you hear the frightful Dutch and see their mouths distorted by its disgusting accents. We have very little communication with the navy, probably owing to a little jalousy caused by the un-settled prize money.

Earlier in the same epistle Colonel Harness says that he finds " the navy begin to see the justice " of the army's claims to share the Soldanha prize money; so we may hope that the " little jalousy " speedily evaporated. Whether this money was ever received the letters curiously do not reveal.

On 15 October he found time to write another long letter giving further impressions of his surroundings.

Good Hope

I have never given you any account of this place. In short I know not where to begin without writing a history. This town is very regularly built, the streets all drawn in straight lines, and a handsome square in the centre. The houses from the street look almost magnificent—certainly much more attention is given to ornament them on the outside than within. The inhabitants are very dressy and fond of show. They are governed by their old laws. A Fiscal is the Chief Magistrate. General Craig never interferes in their decisions, and from a very particular regard he has always paid to their interests in all disputes between Natives and Europeans, as well as from the full liberty he has left them in with regard to market and merchandizes, he has gained the most deserved popularity. Colonel Aston has just returned from a tour he has been making up the country of about a hundred miles. In going ten miles you have almost all the variety this Country affords. Immense Mountains and intermediate valleys, with farm houses interspersed at some miles distance from each other, surrounded with small cultivated spots, their large droves of cattle dispersed and ranging all over the country. The at least twenty thousand additional people they have now to feed, the Navy, increased army and Dutch prisoners of war, create a general bustle.

This is the season for bringing in the wine, so that the streets are full of waggons, each drawn by sixteen oxen. Some of them came six weeks journey from the country. The farmer and his slaves live in the waggons during this time, or stop at the several houses they meet with on the way; but the more ordinary mode is to let out the oxen to graze whenever they meet with a spring. The oxen are much lighter made than the European, and trot along very fast. A cord is fastened to the horns of the two leaders, which a slave takes hold of and runs before them. Most of the inhabitants of the town have farms in the country. Barley is more prized than wheat, oats are not grown but by one or two gentlemen. Our horses are fed with the green barley, which as soon as it is in ear is mown for that purpose. This is cut short and the old barley mixed with it. It makes them uncommonly fat. They get two crops of this unripe barley in a year. I have not seen any hay in the country. The Dutch have been in the custom of treating the poor Hottentots with such rigour that to find they are not insulted or ill-treated raises their adoration. The General has had several deputations lately from the Caffres. They are of a blacker tint than the Hottentots and of a stouter race. They possess very large herds of cattle which they bring in for sale. I saw two of their chiefs throw their dart which they do with great dexterity. We gave them some old buttons, the most acceptable present to these *great men*. Several Whiskeys and light carriages have been brought out, and are caught at with great avidity. It is wonderful to see with what address the slaves drive eight horses at a full gallop. You are aware that they are not much larger than English ponies. Their whips are many yards long.

The price of every article is rising in a degree beyond belief. The wine which sold for fifteen dollars a barrel a year ago now sells for fifty. The quantity which is brought into the town exceeds calculation. With pains and a certain market, and unfettered from the monopoly of the Dutch East India Company, there is reason to look forward to very considerable improvement in the Wine of the Cape. This settlement is in so very infant a state, and has been so *courvee'd* by the Dutch Company, there is reason to see all the advantages that may be expected from its climate and relative situation. Of course at this moment it has no staple article of commerce. I am sorry to find that the wheat that has been sent home is full of the weevil, and from thence unfit for seed. I learn from the gentlemen who understand these things best here, that a bushel of Cape wheat weighs many pounds heavier than that measure of English—or indeed European. Everything committed to the soil is said to be reproduced in lavish abundance. I can conceive the same thing would not happen in the same proportion if the Settlement were better peopled, as now the farmer has his choice of spots which he burns the surface off, and running over it with his plough, scatters about his seed and waits for the harvest, for a sure crop without further trouble. The spots about this town are very pretty, well wooded gardens with walks shaded by myrtle hedges and orange trees and very fine vineyards around them.

Letters arrived from home, but with little regularity. " It is so very long since I heard from you ", he says rather pathetically in the middle of November; and five days later he feels " happiness unspeakable " when no less than four letters arrive in one packet.

19 November

Two were given me yesterday as I was going to dinner. I could not eat a bit. The other two were brought me at the parade. I read them at breakfast. Poor Colonel Ramsey grew quite gruff, he asked me for twenty things, without my attending to one; at last he got up and said he must help himself, for he saw I was absent.

During the greater part of the four months that the regiment spent—on the whole not unpleasantly ("We were very gay while the Fleet remained")—at the Cape, Colonel Harness was hoping for and fully expecting an early return to England. But there came disappointment. In the same letter of 19 November, which began so happily, he broke the news of a longer separation.

My beloved wife General St Leger has just informed me that we go with him to Madras. Bear my angel with fortitude and love this dispensation. It is heaven that guides and protects. Never have I absented myself one instant from you but what Duty *and Love* have urged. This is the *last separation we will undergo*.

The day before the regiment embarked he put the brighter side of the picture.

Cape Town, 7 December 1796

I told you the civilities I experience from my old Friend General St Leger, and that he has succeeded in getting the Regt to Madras. My adored wife our separation shall not be greatly lengthened. The advantages are enormous. My *additional pay* will be Sixty Pounds a Month, and probably a Command. How will our present pain be amply rewarded. It is our last separation. Heaven will reward our exertions, and our prosperity, *our Children's* prosperity will sweeten even absence.

The last letter of the South African series, written on 23 December, while passing by Madagascar, told of a pleasant voyage.

I never was so comfortable on board Ship. We live uncommonly well and everything is in the same good order as in a Gentleman's House on shore. We sit down eighteen, very Gentlemanlike men with four well behaved young Ladies.

7

Marking Time in Ceylon

WILLIAM HARNESS was destined to spend much of his military service sojourning on islands, while awaiting events—Guernsey, the barren Ile de Yeu, and now nearly two years in Ceylon. After a fleeting stay of five days in Madras the regiment set sail for the recently acquired port of Trincomali.

Trincomali, 16 March 1797

After a voyage of fifteen days, but which it often takes but a day and a half to effect, we came to an anchor in this Port of the Island of Ceylon on the 13th. We found continual delays from foul winds, calm, and contrary currents. We had seven Companies on board the Fairlie and when we arrived, after retrenching the poor fellows of their water to the shortest allowance, we had but two Casks remaining. In working into the Harbour we struck upon a rock; but through the skill and activity of our Captain the Ship was soon got off, and without material injury. Colonel Champagné has the civil and military Command of this Port, beautiful Harbour and Country for two Hundred miles. The men of the 72nd Regiment have been unhealthy here, although the Officers have found it much otherwise. Colonel Fraser, whom Colonel Champagné relieves, has benefited the air much by cutting down the woods and improving the Barracks. A few abuses remain to be corrected and I doubt not but our people will preserve good health. The Island is famous for its fine air. It is said to have been the residence of Adam after the Fall. The highest mountain is called Adam's Mountain. Would to God my Bessy were with me. I have a very snug pretty house with a long range of Offices. Poultry yard &c with Orange and other Fruit Trees, with a pretty octagon sort of summer house of two stories at the end of my premises, looking to the sea and in every direction. The supper room is very pretty indeed. It is here I write to the dearest friend this world can give me; and here I tell her my present pay is one hundred pounds per month, and that every farthing of it I can possibly spare from the heavy expenses I am obliged to incur shall be a sacred deposit to participate with the cherished partner of my life and *our own* children.

Colonel Ramsey commands at Fort Canaburg with two Companies. Col Champagné has given up the Command of the 8 Companies that are here to me. In taking possession of a country so new you will imagine I have much to do.

Like the Cape of Good Hope, Ceylon, or rather part of Ceylon, had been captured from the Dutch in 1795. The British now possessed the low-lying land round the coast, but the sovereignty of the island was divided. The mountainous country in the interior was still held, as it had been held in independence for three hundred years while European peoples came and went upon the coastal region, by the King of Kandy and his native people. They were a trying race to have as neighbours, suspicious, conceited, and very difficult to approach or to trade with. Early in 1803 negotiations with this rather impossible potentate broke down and for over two years a minor, inglorious, and ineffective war was carried on. It was not until 1815 that the whole of the island came under British rule.

Save for the lengthening and heart-rending separation from his wife and children and the slow and infrequent arrival of letters from home, Colonel Harness found these years in Ceylon on the whole pleasant and interesting. He enjoyed his horse exercise in the early morning and the cool of the evening— " I am on horseback every morning a good half hour before sunrise ". He enjoyed too the new and varied experiences. On 2 April 1797 he wrote a long letter describing his life and surroundings and giving some reminiscences of his short stay at Madras.

Trincomali, 2 April 1797
Three Indiamen have come to an anchor in this Harbour. They are waiting to be joined by three from Madras and

Calcutta to proceed to England. I shall have a delightful opportunity to write by them. Sir Ralph Abercrombie, our late Commander in Chief, is on board; nobody is yet come on shore. I find nothing in the air, or water, or in short the Elements that can with proper attention render this place unhealthy. Situated at 8 degrees from the Line you would suppose the heat must be excessive, but fortunately we have the sea breeze, which cools the air from nine o'Clock in the morning. I will tell my Bessy how I pass my day here. Zamor (who is well and all he should be) comes into my room as soon as the morning gun fires, and I immediately get up, at half past five and walk round the garrison. At six attend the Regimental Parade, at half past the public Guards march off, at 7 three or four Gentlemen return with me to breakfast. At 9 I go to my little Room, and read, write, or transact Regimental business till 12, when I take a crust of Bread and a glass of madiera. From one to three I sleep, and at four dine. At six the Evening parade and exercise; after that make visits or receive them; soon after nine retire to bed. In this climate you see how much rest is required. Nobody moves out from nine to three but on business. The houses are calculated admirably for coolness, and sitting without motion you are not aware of the intense heat without. Wishing to save for us as much as possible I keep but five servants. Colonel Champagné has twenty-nine, and I sometimes think I am better served.

Our fruits are plantains, shaddocks, the cocoa nut and a variety of others of uncouth shapes and names. In the Garrison we have two Regiments of Sepoys. It is surprising to see with what exact regularity they go through their Duty. The Black Town is just across the Esplanade, the houses are but of one story, very miserable, and each in the centre of a garden enclosed within a high hedge. They are almost without Cloathing, and rice is their chief food. They are very numerous. It is wonderful that people whose wants are so few will condescend to drudge in the heat of the sun in the meanest occupation. They are very ingenious. Give them but a pattern and there is nothing they will not execute. They have scarcely any furniture. A few earthen pots baked in the sun, and a knife make almost the total of it. The Harbour is full of choicest fish, and Turtle so plenty that it is served out to the Soldiers.

Cattle is said to have risen to three times its usual price. I have a beautiful Cow and Calf which I gave the enormous sum of three Pagodas for; a pagoda is eight shillings. You get sixteen fowls for a pagoda. We were told at Madras we should find nothing here to eat, and that the water was yellow and unwholesome. I never saw finer. At so short a distance to know so little is to be accounted for but in one way, which is that everybody conspires to keep the Government in the dark. It is on the scarcity and dearness of every article that at Trincomali we have double allowances. Our Mess Table is plentifully and elegantly supplied, including an unlimited quantity of Porter for ten Pagodas per month. Madiera is the usual wine and is drunk under two shillings the Bottle. Claret is drunk on Sundays and Thursdays, two public days on which we see our friends.

General Sir Ralph Abercrombie came ashore and breakfasted with Colonel Champagné this morning. He is going home to repose on his honours and an excellent fortune.[1]

I have said nothing of this place. I have been but once out of the Fort, when I accompanied Colonel Champagné to the Black Town. I hear there are large herds of wild Elephants within two miles and Birds of the most beautiful plumage. The Pearl Fishery is carried on to great extent. The shore abounds in curious shells. I am sorry I have no knowledge in them or it would be worth while to make a Collection. The precious metals and all kinds of precious stones are productions of this Island. You see the Natives with very large holes in their Ears and several large pieces of gold passing through them, that force down the ears to a frightful length. Even the water carriers are not without them. The women have great Quantities around their necks. Bars of gold and silver round

---

[1] Far from " reposing on his honours " this wise, upright old soldier was to die of wounds received in battle after a successful landing in Egypt. Fortescue thus describes him: " Though delighting to the end in Livy and Cicero, in Caesar and Tacitus, and though familiar with all that was best in contemporary literature, Abercrombie was essentially a thinker rather than a reader. . . . No matter what impossibilities Ministers might require of him, no matter how distasteful their projects to his feelings or how repugnant to his judgment, he was always ready to take their orders and to do his best. He did not lack the courage to point out the fatuity of their plans, nor to protest against them . . . but when once the decision of the Cabinet was taken, he accepted it with unswerving loyalty." *A History of the British Army*, Vol. 4, Book XII, p. 844.

their arms and wrists with large rings on the Toes. They are strict observers of the Religious customs of the Castes, in which are included the most extravagant prejudices. There is a species of large hawke which they in some degree worship and which they hold it is a crime to hurt. The consequence is that even in the very fort at Madras you are annoyed by these overgrown pests, that hover about you by flocks and continually take away provisions out of the children's hands.

Our Servants will eat nothing of which we have fed or even touched. We brought some from Madras, and while on board ship the situation of those poor fellows was afflicting. For three days several of them would not touch a drop of water after all they had laid in for themselves was out. Had we remained longer at sea they would have died rather then have drunk of the water that has been touched by one not of their own Cast. A Gentoo [1] was sleeping with his mouth open upon the deck, and one of our young men very boyishly poured some wine into his mouth. Poor fellow, he awoke in torment, and I can fancy his spirits have never recovered their tone. He is Colonel Champagenés Second Dubash. Your head Dubash furnishes everything you want; your second is a kind of valet who will dress hair, and wait at table. The Mitta cleans Shoes and exercises the lower offices. For every horse you have two Men, a Grass-Cutter [2] and the feeder. At Madras I was obliged to have a Palankeen and nine bearers which I do without here. I have been obliged to raise Zamor's wages to thirty guineas a year. I was led to regard as the accounts of Travellers those they gave me of the rate and distance the Palankeen Bearers would take a person in a day. I thought in a burning climate it was impossible these poor people would take you in a carriage, far from light, fifty miles in a day, but I find they will exceed it for several days together. The Palankeen is a narrow long post Chaise without wheels. I mean Built in the same manner, the roof is not so high. It is about five feet in

[1] Hindu.

[2] In another letter Colonel Harness describes the duties of this man: " The Grass-Cutter carrys the nosebag and Head and heel ropes. He has an instrument [that] looks like a small chopping Knive but with the handle two feet long. With this he cuts up the grass by the roots; when well washed the Roots are said to be the most nutricious part."

107

length. You lie along with a backboard to support the upper part of the Body. They are beautifully painted and varnished, and have lamps in the front. Mine had three, with a silver bead round the leather. You are carried by four Men at a time who change every three minutes. They sing as they run along which keeps them in the same step and time.

It was the Race week when we landed at Madras. The races were at the Mount five miles from us. I did not go. The style of the Tables are very elegant. The Wine is I conceive rendered unwholesome by the extreme of cold they give it. It freezes you. I was told it costs my Lord Hobart fifteen hundred pounds a year to cool his wine. The mode is very expensive. Here when you dine out your servant always carries your chair.

The surf at Madras is so high and beats with that violence that a European Boat would be dashed to pieces in attempting to land. You are therefore landed by the Natives in their Boats which it is frightful to enter, they appear so ill-constructed and of such miserable materials. They are sewn together, not having a single nail throughout. They will take twenty people in them. You see the water bursting in in every part, and it is the diligent occupation of one man to keep it under. The End where you stand is strewed two or three feet deep with bushes to keep you dry. At the full of the moon each boat is attended by two or three Katamarans (two logs of wood fastened together) on each of which sit two Blacks poising themselves, and directing them through the most stormy seas with great dexterity. I never was fond of Boating, and committed to such a frail machine, with the Surf that appeared ready to break us to pieces every instant I felt a perfect Coward, and constantly looked in my friend Captain Kemp's countenance to gather our fate. We had no rudder, and the oars or paddles are as miserable as the Boat. The naked Blacks that rowed us, making the most hideous noise, and watching every wave with their Eyes turned up, heightened the scene. They are most uncommonly expert and frightful as it at first appears, accidents are very rare.

At Madras are made the very fine linens for Shirts &c. I bought several pieces, as well as coloured linens, and two handsome Palampose [1] or coverings for the Bed. It surprised me

[1] A kind of chintz bedcover.

to find the articles of one Presidency as dear at another as they would be in England. And China at Madras is nearly as dear as in London—dearer than at Dover or Guernsey. They told me it was impossible to do without a table set. I bought one, but finding our mess so comfortable and Col. C without, I was happy to part with it to him—reflecting on the Madness of a Man with a beloved Wife and three dear Children giving dinners when he can so well return the kindnesses of his friends at the Mess. The beds here are very comfortable. The Bottom is white broad Tape intertwined so close as to have no opening; the Matrasses are the best in the world. The curtains of very fine white Muslin with an Inner Curtain of green gauze, which tucks in all round to keep out the muskitoes. It is customary to sleep in Muskito Trousers which go over the feet and come up very high, tying round the waist. The first night the feel was very odd.

We have a report here that the Empress of Russia is dead, that Spain has declared war and that Admiral Mann is blocked up at Gibraltar. I fear my Brother is not yet returned to England. How much will it surprise him to find where I am, but not more than it does me.

More ships are come round. They will probably not remain long here. I see a great many natives about Colonel C.'s door. One presented him with a beautiful Topaz ring; others brought him two Elephant's teeth, kissed his Foot, and told him if he would lend him a tame Elephant he would catch him wild ones. I see one with a large fan that rests on the ground and the other end spreads over the man's Head. One has a very large Deer, a third Poultry. There are several Baskets of Birds, and a charming spotted Fawn; Tyger skins. Colonel F. was very unpopular, they are much pleased with the change. I see a wild Hog among the group. The meat is very fine. The Deceptions and sleight of hand are very curious. I was much disgusted with seeing one of these Conjurors swallow a Sword of at least half a yard long, of real steel and without any trick. They turn live snakes of eight or nine feet long, after winding them round their bodies in the oddest manner, into Pidgeons which fly and settle round them. Breslaw [1] and his competitors

[1] This famous conjuror published in 1784 a little book of tricks, *Breslaw's Last Legacy*, which went into several editions.

in England would have much to learn from these crafty black Gentry. The wild Peacock is a beautiful bird, I see them very often at table.

It is very pleasant taking exercise in the cool of the Evening. I think I have told you this is the finest Harbour in India. A Thousand ships could ride in it in the utmost security. It is, as the Seamen express it, so well land-locked. The Entrance is very well defended by Fort Ostenburg which is situated on the opposite point. It is surprising how it could fall so easily into our hands. During the Monsoon all the Navy took shelter here. It is supposed my Lord Hobart, and all the Naval people, look upon it to be of infinitely greater consequence than the Cape of Good Hope. They are all writing strong representations of its importance to the East India Company and seem to think it will be made a point to keep it at the peace. Among the trees I think the Tulip Tree the most beautiful, it is very large and umbrageous with a flower resembling the Tulip.

You will have alter'd our dear Charles's Dress before this reaches you, Dear good boy, I suppose he reads now like a man, and that he and little Jane pronounce every word with as much propriety as their Mama.

What a jumble of a letter is this. You will see, my Bessy, how my thoughts fly. I write them as they start without method or arrangement.

The insignificant number of servants that her husband employed evidently made a painful impression on the Colonel's lady.

It hurts me [wrote Elizabeth] that you should have but five servants when Colonel Champagné has twenty-nine; and I fear you do not always find yourself *better served*. I recollect that the Colonel's pride was not in parade and show when at Hilsey and do you not remember the *Sentry*? From that I conclude that he finds a great number necessary, and I will hope to be told in your next that you, my H., have a *few* more— and of every thing else in proportion. You have sacrificed too much already to your Wife and dear Children.

In July there was a desolate *cri du coeur* from Ceylon:

> Trincomali, 25 July

It is now nearly ten Months since I heard from you, the longest period of unhappiness I ever knew arise from this painful cause. When I left you I had no idea our separation would have been for so long a term as what I have past without hearing one word from you. I am satisfied Reams of paper must be scattered about the world in search of the Regimt; there are many Officers who have not seen the scratch of a Pen from their nearest Friends since we left England. The last of yours, my beloved Wife, is the 29th Sept. A Fleet is arrived at Madras but the Ship which had the letters on board separated at sea. Another Ship came in here two days ago from Bombay with two Boxes of letters on board from the Cape, but the Boxes were sealed and directed to Madras. After her arrival there the Tapall (or Post) takes twelve or thirteen days to come here. Ships from Europe are put into Calcutta.

The letter ends in more cheerful vein with an account of a " little dinner " that rivals those of Parson Woodeforde.

> My Bessy on the 20th I gave a most comfortable little dinner to six Friends. Fish, Soup, Roast Veal with white mince under it, Pigeon Pye, Fricasee Chicken (Maintenon), Cutlets in cover'd dishes, Mouton au Gratin, Potatoes, Stewed Spinage, Roast Duck and a Pudding and a handsome Dessert. Porter, Madeira and Claret. Col. Champagné, Col. Ramsey, Paymaster Genl, Chief Engineer and Commanding Officer of artillery. My Betsy if I have said more of this than a Dinner deserves, remember it was given on *your Birthday*, which with that of our marriage, I mean wedding day, are the only times I have given dinners since I have been in India, and the occasions will justify the detail. Again My Betsy would not dislike to know what this Island could furnish.

That the island did not furnish every necessity of life is shown by a request that Bessy should send out " two Dozen Tooth Brushes for me; there is no doing without them ".

The strain of separation was equally felt at home. During

her husband's " longest period of unhappiness " Elizabeth was
writing of little Charles:

He has just been upstairs and says " pray Mama tell Papa
to come home; tell him there is Peace and I am sure he will
begin to come home to-morrow ". Then poor little Jane echoes
[him]. Charles examined your picture and asked me if I
thought it very much like Papa, and with a mournful voice
said, " Mama I hardly remember Papa's face, but I very well
remember watching him down the lane when he went away ".

Small unknown Jemima was " very much like dear Charles ",
a lively baby, and her mother foresaw that " she will have a
great deal of drollery about her ".

In August 1797 William's heart was gladdened by receiving
five letters within three days, " the last dated 13th February ".
With his mind always full of plans for the future, when service
abroad should be ended, Colonel Harness's thoughts turned at
this time to a project for settling for two years in the South
of France. " What a charming place the South of France and
how happy an one for the Education of our Children. Would
to God I could commence it." And in another letter, " I am
charmed with the idea of taking our dear Children to France
for a couple of years. It would be very advantageous to them.
I let my imagination lead me into those charming fields of
hoped future happiness and it cheers the absence I am doomed
to endure." (How different was that war from those we in
our day have experienced! What British officer serving in 1916
or in 1940 would have thought it either possible or desirable
to make plans for taking his family to the enemy country for
their education?)

He sent small presents home when he was able to find anything worth the sending—a shawl for " kind Aunty Croke ",
some native pictures given him by a friend, in which " the
figures are frightful, but the colours are beautiful "; shells for
the children, muslin for his wife, and " a Ring with the different
stones of this Island "; bead necklaces for the little girls. " I
fancy Jane and my little Bessy will look very pretty in necklaces
of the beads you will find in the box." And again, " I have a
piece of Cloath I brought with me from Madras intending it

for Shirts, but I have taken it into my head you could do something with it, perhaps in the Frocks way, for our dear little Girls, and I should like them to have something of Papa's."

Now that William Harness was in charge of eight companies of the regiment he was much concerned with the health of his men.

Trincomallie, 17 August 1797

It is with pleasure I find the Regimt growing healthy daily. We suffered considerably the first three months. Imprudence, a burning sun and bad barrack and a total change of diet, destitute of all the assistants given to European Regiments and unskillful of the resources of the Country, our mortality may be traced from causes very foreign to the climate. Colonel Champagné has cut down all the underwood of the neighbourhood, and I have racked my poor brains for sources of comfort and health. It is with real pleasure I can say that not a single Officer is sick and that the Men are as healthy as any Regimt in England. On taking the Command of the Regimt the first thing I did was to punish severely and to hold as infamous and base the ill-treating of the Islanders, and gave it in orders that the Soldiers should observe it is only by gentleness and kind treatment the Natives can be encouraged to bring into them the several articles of provisions and Comfort they may stand in need of; that by observing such conduct they would soon see their wants plentifully and of course cheaply supplyed; that should the Soldier conceive any inclination in the Inhabitants to cheat or overreach him, he was expressly forbid to redress himself, but in all cases to refer to his Officers who would see justice done him. I am happy to say my wishes have proved successful.

Two months later he was still able to give a good report.

8 October 1797

The Regiment is quite as healthy as it is probable they would be in England; but the eternal care and almost privation it requires to preserve health is more than our young men will always undergo. Those who have taken a moderate care

113

of so valuable a good have been amply repaid. Whenever I have seen an inclination to sit over the bottle I have as constantly ordered my horse.

Colonel Harness showed as much care for the moral as for the physical health of the young officers under him.

17 August 1797

One day is very like another. I ride in the morning and in the Evening we have established a Meeting at each others houses, and play cards for small sums, with wine and water and Segars. I am at home every tuesday Evening. Every Body come without invitation. We light up the Viranda at 7 o'clock and no game is began after nine. I saw a frightful flame of gambling lighting up among the young men and instituted this Meeting to check it, which it has effected. We spread five card Tables. These meetings are very sociable and attach the Officers to each other.

In September 1797 the Colonel sent his wife a copy of the sick returns and a very favourable report on the health of the 80th Regiment—a report which reflects great credit both on Dr Christie, the Medical Officer, and on Colonel Harness himself—more especially in view of the immense difficulties under which their work was carried on. Fevers, flux, and swelling are some of the disorders mentioned.

Is it to be wondered at, that of between eight and nine hundred soldiers who drink of the vilest spirits, the worst of arrack, *ten* should be fluxt, and six should have injured their livers; but they continue to get a still more pernicious drink called Toddy, altho interdicted by the severest assurances of punishment to the Soldier, and, when discouraged by the loss of the whole wood in which it is produced, to the native Vendor. It is obtained by cutting off the young Cocoa nut, as soon as the appearance of formation is discovered, and hanging an earthen pot to receive the juice issuing from the stork. This liquor, altho said to be wholesome in the morning, after the sun has, for a few hours, shone on it, ferments and takes a most intoxicating quality. It is utterly impossible to keep the

Soldiers from it. The women bring it into the Fort under their clothes. The Swelling is a disorder said to be, peculiarly, almost confined to this Island. It had proved very fatal to the Regt we relieved. On our coming we lost nearly thirty men by it, it began at the feet, and rapidly spread upwards untill in a very short period it gained the vital parts. It was supposed to be almost constantly fatal, and had proved so. To Christie's honor we now never lose a man by it. When we take into the account the debauched habits of the Soldier, with the night duties he is obliged to undergo, in a Climate so different from his own, I declare for my own part I am struck with wonder at the healthiness of the Regiment. The Officers go out shooting in the Sun, and take liberties with their constitutions that prudence disavows, still it is an uncommon thing for an Officer to absent himself from the Mess through want of health. As to myself I have as good as I ever enjoyed.

In spite of the " little dinners " twice a year Colonel Harness's mind was continually occupied with thoughts of economies that he could make for the greater comfort of his family and as a means towards realizing that rosy future in his own home of which he so constantly dreamed. The letter of 17 August continues:

Should we succeed in the Soldanah prize money, of which few doubts are entertained, I trust we should soon be comfortable. Colonel Champagné is growing very rich here. I shall be leaving the East just as I may expect a Command but my Bessy will excuse me, and unless the means of getting money are very different from what they are here, believe me I shall very little regret it. The most abject meanness is attached to it. The Commandant allows but one Butcher to kill meat, who makes him a monthly present, but one Baker, but one person to sell spirits &c &c &c. The consequent extortion and vile articles is but the least of the evil. Col. C. follows but what is called the custom of the Country as he found it established.

We get another glimpse of the faithful Zamor.

Zamor is well. I had a little trouble with him for a short time. The Natives are anxious to get European Servants out of the country and will not attend to their directions. I fancyed too that Zamor was desirous of quitting it. I believed his zeal was slackened, but he came about on my speaking to him and told me he would endeavour every thing to preserve my good opinion. He is always in the way and I never yet saw him drunk. You know the care he takes of my property. He is in fact a treasure. He teachs the little Walches [1] French. He plays the Fiddle five hours a day at least, but sees that everything is done.

7 January 1798

We are so completely out of the world that nothing is to be had but money. I spend as little of mine as possible and am affraid looked upon as rather shabby. I told Colonel Champagné yesterday that I was living on the soul of my Boot. That if I had not the most dear and tender connexions that rendered economy a Duty I should consider the manner in which I see some men live here not only as a want of taste but as completely senseless; for surely no reasonable being could allow himself to squander away in a country like this the means of lasting comfort and respectability at home.

9 March 1798

I have reduced my expenses to eighty Pagodas a month out of two hundred and fifty.

Elizabeth evidently felt that her husband's economies went too far, for in August 1798 he wrote to dispel her disquietude.

My dearest Bessy wishes me to keep more servants, but I have every thing necessary to comfort. I even sometimes think I am wronging you with two Horses and a Gigg; but, my Bessy, we have no taxes here and the first is the only expense. I give no dinners but return all those I receive at the Mess, where I see every Body that it is necessary to see, and I hope

---

[1] James, one of the " little Walches ", the children of a fellow-officer, was sent home the following year to go to school in England, where he was under the watchful care of Elizabeth Harness. He became the close friend of Charles.

116

with a look of liberality. The Admirals, all the Captains of the Fleet, and every Officer of it I know. The Admiral says it is the only Gentlemanlike Mess he knows, he is never asked to drink more wine than he likes, he has always as much as he likes, and whenever he wishes to leave the table Zamor has Coffee ready at my Quarters. In all my expenses I do not exceed the pay of a Lieutenant. I really am not growing jewish, but I feel a pain in expending a Pagoda unnecessarily. The thermometer is at Ninety two. When shall I enjoy the cool comfortable of September in England.

On 26 December 1797 William Harness began another very long descriptive letter which did not finish until 22 May.

Your last of the 25th April I received but three weeks ago. Your delightful account of our dear Children is most tenderly gratifying. I long to see Charles in his new dress, and to hear him read, and my little brown Jane. Charmingly has our unseen Bessy recovered from the small Pox. I long to tell you when we leave this Island which we expect to be told every day. I now understand we are to go to the Coast and it is believed very soon, that is to say as soon as the present Monsoon ceases. We were led to apprehend that it would be impossible to stir out of our houses for four or five days together, that the wind blew from the four quarters at once and that no covering of any house was secure. It certainly rained more than usual but the Monsoon is nearly over, and there has been but two days I have not taken my usual rides, and on no day have I been confined to my house. The season is cooler than we have found any other. I bear a counterpain on my bed and wear a Kersemere waistcoat in the morning. This day the sun has been obscured and I have been with the Engineer fixing on a place to encamp on the Hill as soon as the blowing weather is over; for should we stay but a month I see so much advantage in the air of the Hill and Sea breeze that I am determined to encamp the Regiment.

Christmas day is a very great holiday here. When I got up yesterday I found the House stuck with plantain trees and two large ones full of Fruit and dressed out with flowers at my Door. The floors were all strewed with Rushes, aromatic leaves and flowers. The Black people all bring presents, large groops danced in the street. We had the whole Garrison to dine with us.

From Trincomallie I went on a pleasant party given by Captain and Mrs Norris to the Hot Wells distant about seven miles. The Seven wells are enclosed by a wall and are apparently the production of one Spring although perfectly separate at the surface. The water we found at 110 Degrees Heat. From the Wells issues a hot stream and, taking a winding direction in the wood, returns at about a hundred yards distance in a smooth easy current of about nine feet broad. Here it is conducted by two spouts approaching each other till you can reach them, when you are surprized to find the water conveyed immediately from the same current hot to your right hand and cold to your left. It is presumable that the water issuing from the hot spring is joined in its passage through the wood by another small but cold current and running but a small distance together they are received into the spouts before they have time to coalesce.

The Natives are abundantly superstitious and recount tales of the origin and efficacy of the Wells that indicate the most fertile Imagination as well as strong biass to delusion. At the spot, which is romantically fitted for all the wild mazes of superstition, besides two Chowthies [1] erected by benevolence for accomadation of Travellers, there is an ancient Pagoda dedicated to the uninspired religion of the Heart—to those Gods that Fear, Gratitude, Love, wonder, filial piety and erratic Fancy have engendered. A small chamber at the entrance furnishes all the habitation of a Bramin whose real piety may be measured from his privations and poverty. For the lengthy period of thirty years his seclusion from the social Comforts has bared his bones. The faithful Victim of a sound heart and a frail head, he heaped story upon story and ran down the history of these wonder-working Wells to seven Virgins who take up their watery abode in, and preside over, them. In front of the Pagoda grows a lofty and spreading Mango Tree, the largest it is said on the Island. A native told me from this Tree drops every day at 12 o'Clock a ripe Fruit for God Almighty, that on solemn occasions he gives it to his favourite Bramin, who eats it for him. Another told me he

---

[1] Probably Choultries—an inn or place for reception of travellers.

comes out every year on a certain day to meet his Father who has been dead these ten years. He has never seen him but knows he is on that day near the spot and feels a pleasure to be near him.

The Kite is sacred among them. There are fixt days they come out in tribes to scatter rice for the Bramin Kites. The artless energy with which you are told the most incredible things manifests the fervor and steadfastness of their Belief. This spot is highly venerated and very distant pilgrimages, as well as costly offerings, are made to it. The road to it is cut through a lofty wood and is in many places so completely over-hung by the interlacing of Bows that you are obliged to dismount. It is perfectly impervious to a tropical meridian sun. The Trees afford much to catch an European eye unused to see the Trunks dividing into three or four separate bodies, and, wreathing preposterously their serpentine courses again, unite in a solid whole, and repeating their whimsocal distortion to their very summits. The Banyan Tree could not have escaped notice. After reading the scarcely to be credited accounts I was struck with its view, its towering height, wide streaching branches, umbrageous leaves and thick knotty roots descending many an airy fathom and fibrating as they approach to catch the soil. The first seen variegation of plumage, new shape, new sounds of the feathered inhabitants, the Tracks of Elephants, the unknown crys of unknown animals, the glimpse of others frisking across the road left almost to the Imagination to fashion the trace, but half remembered, and no correspondant likeness in the fancy for assimilation. The Shrubs, leaves, flowers, reptiles, insects, the beetles and very flys that buz by the astonished ear, all all distract. Creation is new, all is change.

The sudden break in the wood presents at a short distance a ridge of rocks tumbled upon one another in all the disorder of nature oppressed, and seems as if cast from another world. Arrived at the magic spot the least of your surprize would not perhaps be raised by the Hospitality of our Host; To see a Table plentifully and elegantly covered, with French Wines, English ales and Porter, Coffee &c and all the comforts of an English entertainment. Seeing no Kitchen I could not help asking how was the ham so nicely boiled, where was the Turkey roasted and the fine saddle of mutton, the Soup, the Fish, the ducks, the made dishes how dressed, the chicken pye and Tarts how so well baked, and all served up so hot with hot water plates. How brought out the dining and Card Tables, Chairs, China for breakfast, dinner and dessert with all the " Batterie de cuisine " at that distance through the wood without carriage or Horses; how every thing ready, nothing wanted forgotten. It is wonderful in this Country with what ease all these difficulties are smoothed away or rather how they disappeared before the just organisation, as the French would call it, of our generous Friends. Among my airy visions I sometimes hope I may have the pleasure of introducing them to you. They talk of going to England to educate their children. Mrs N. has never been there.

On New Year's Day Colonel Champagné gave what is described with truth as a " great dinner " to " the marryed People ". " He has what will surprize you *two Turtles*, a Goose a Turkey, a fat Sheep and I have sent him a fine calf. You see our fare will be solid."

William Harness's kindly understanding sympathy with the victims of " a sound heart and a frail head " was shown in another incident which he recorded in the following year—for they had not left for the Indian coast as he had expected.

25 August 1798

You have heard, my Bessy, of the voluntary and severe punishments the Indians impose on themselves by distorting themselves &c, till their limbs take the most unnatural form. I yesterday saw a man with a very large Iron frame like a window frame with three bars every way and rivetted by a collar round his neck, so that he could not possibly lie down. I took the measure of it each way with my cane. He told me that he had had it on upwards of three years and had made a vow not to take it off untill he had collected enough money to erect a temple to his God. He came to ask leave to cut some stones from a Rock. I thought I was not committing an act offensive to the God of Mercy in giving a few shillings to assist in getting this poor deluded good man out of real torture. He told me he had collected above 3,000 Rupees which I hoped would build a most magnificent abode for his Swammey.[1]

[1] *Swami*—a Hindu idol.

With the " poor deluded " Hindus he could sympathise, but for the Malay soldiers Colonel Harness had no good word. In the same long letter that told of the expedition to the Hot Wells he wrote with much distaste of these irregulars:

We have a Corps here of Malays, of irregular Troops. They were in the Dutch service and, taken at this place, they have been prevailed on to enter into the Companies Service. Like all Malays they are of the most implacable and revengeful disposition. A dispute arose yesterday between some of them and some artillery Lascars, when they drew their Creeses and killed two poor Lascars on the spot, and wounded several others. Their Creeses are wavey, of an extraordinary temper. They are the property of the Soldiers and made by them. They are buryed in the earth for a length of time with a composition of the most venimous herbs and other poisonous substances; of the solid part that remains are these frightful instruments fashioned. At the Capture of this place the Malays made a sortie from the fort and surprized an advanced Guard and creesed every one of them. The night was obscure and their colour and prostrate position, for they crawled on their hands and feet, were all circumstances that Troops unused to their irregular advances could but weakly guard themselves against. They returned to the fort unhurt. This was the most fatal business of the seige. They are the strongest race of people I ever heard of, and the ugliest. They possess in an eminent degree the Talent of entrapping and taking alive the wild and obnoxious animals. They are excellent fishermen, have a great knack of rearing poultry. They enter the woods and return laden with fruits, herbs and animals. The good natured and fearful Inhabitants are petrifyed at the sight of them. They are the most consumate thieves in the world. They burrow at a distance and remove trunks &c out of the Chamber and from under your bed. Gaming is their ruling passion. They will stake their Children on a throw. They are extremely jealous notwithstanding they have each three or four wives. I know no race of men to possess so few virtues or so strong and numerous vices. How unlike the pious and sober Bramins who you know will eat of nothing that ever drew Life! Perhaps it is an excess of humanity, but at all events it is so aimable a weakness that it flatters the vanity of the most hard hearted among us, and what we have not the power to practice we have not the resolution to condemn.

The tremendous epistle begun on 26 December closes with some messages to Charles and an Indian recipe:

Do tell Charles that I have a very pretty deer spotted all over his Body, with beautifully white Spots running in the most regular Rows, and so tame that he will eat out of our Hand. His Horns are beginning to sprought out. I wish I could send it to my dear little Boy. He would so like to shew it to Jane. I think they would be happy to feed it and then to see it run and frisk and jump and skip about, as nimble as a kitten. It is a beautiful creature. I dare say Charles will think it very droll, but I have a Calf that has been bred up with it, that it has taught to eat rice and biscuit and paper and pocket-handkerchiefs, or my Cloaths if Zamor don't take care of them. The Calf is grown as fat as butter and skips about like the Deer and jumps over him. I am sure he would laugh to see them play together. They are very fond of each other.

The cows here have large humps on their Shoulders which in Bengal are cured in the cold season and barreled up; they are esteemed very fine. The flavor is something like the best part of a Tongue. It is near Twelve o'Clock. I am going to eat mullicatawney with Col. Ramsey; we always eat it every day at that hour. It is a Chicken Broth with the Ingredients that make Curry, gathered Green with Limes Squeezed in it and the juice of the white part of the Cocoa Nut pressed into it. It is very warm and grateful to the Palate.

In the following September his friends, the Norrises, left Ceylon for England. " They are ", wrote William, " by much the most aimable people here and she the only woman I could with pleasure introduce to my own Bessy. They seem to live more like us than any People I know." Years later Colonel and Mrs Norris were to prove good friends to young Charles Harness.

Trimcomallie, 27 September 1798

Captain Norris has just called, he tells me he hopes to leave us immediately and that he has arranged matters to get on board the first Ship he can for Europe. His intelligence has quite surprized me. They are very aimable people, by much the most so of any body here. I shall experience a real loss, for after the noice of the Mess it is quite a retreat to pass an hour there in rational conversation. Mrs N. quite longs to see you. It would not surprize me to hear they had called on you in the tour they talk of making. Detain them a day or two if they do. They can tell you more of this place than any body. Tell Mrs N. you fear I am growing too attached to *Cheroots*. They are the same thing as Segars, or rolls of Tobacco for smooking. She has been frightened lest I should get Norris to smook them. She thinks them very dangerous and sottish. We were strongly recommended to make them in the wet season, as in Holland, and I really believe them to be very wholesome but have never been able to conquor one. I constantly praise them and recommend them to the Soldiers. She has quite beg'd of me to leave them off as they *grow* upon people. It is often the Subject of a Laugh. But do you think, my own Bessy, I shall ever become a smoking, soaking Sott.

News from the European seats of war came through slowly. Admiral Nelson, convinced that the French intended to advance through Egypt to India, spent anxious weeks searching the Mediterranean for signs of their fleet—and won his overwhelming victory at Aboukir on 1 August 1798. Some echoes of his exploits filtered through to Trincomali and William Harness wrote on 22 October:

The Captain of the Intrepid is immediately from Suez, last from Bombay. He says he heard from many of the fugitive Greeks that Admiral Nelson had burnt the Transports that took Buonaparte to Egypt. That had the French acted more secretly there were small craft enough in the red sea to have brought on twenty thousand Troops. That he gave the allarm in every Port and that the sea is now clear. He gives frightful accounts of the plunder of the French.

Meanwhile in India trouble was once more brewing. The cruel and treacherous Tippoo Sahib, Sultan of Mysore, had made peace with the British in 1792, after being compelled by

123

Cornwallis to cede half his dominions to Britain's allies, the Mahratta rulers and the Nizam of Hyderabad. Tippoo himself had in his youth received military training from French officers and at the age of 14 had commanded a corps of cavalry; and he was awaiting his opportunity. It came when Napoleon, all powerful in Europe, turned his mind to the Far East. He found in Tippoo a willing tool, unsubdued and ready for revenge. The invasion of India was not an entirely fantastic notion. French regiments were already in the service of the Nizam of Hyderabad; there were also French soldiers in the Mahratta Confederacy. The French islands of Mauritius and Bourbon were conveniently placed as bases for an invading army. Tippoo was all agog and was already carrying on a secret correspondence with France.

That same year, 1798, the Earl of Mornington (later the Marquis Wellesley), elder brother of the future Iron Duke, became Governor-General of India. He took immediate measures to frustrate France's schemes and persuaded the Nizam to disband his French regiments. Then he turned his undivided attention to Tippoo Sultan.

William Harness in Ceylon regarded this threatening situation lightly.

25 August 1798

We have lately heard that Tippoo was collecting an army and was manifesting dispositions of hostility, but it appears his army was assembled only to assist the collection of his revenue. There does not at present appear the most distant idea of our quitting this Island.

And on 22 October:

It is said that Tippoo has expected assistance from France. I fancy he has been led on by the mad folly of that extravagant nation. We have formed an Army of six thousand men to watch his motions but he is all weakness and poverty. An Officer, a Frenchman too, who the Nizam has taken into his Service to organize his Infantry, has collected a force and, it is reported, has actually set the Nizam at defiance, and republicanized a considerable portion of his Subjects; but I cannot bring myself to believe a Trigger will be drawn in India. An extension of Territory or the promise of plunder have generally determined the Councils of the Honourable Company. The Nizam will perhaps ask the aid of the Marattas.

Nor had Colonel Harness been over-troubled by fears for the safety of England, though at home the thought of invasion was in the air. In August he had written:

I confess I long to hear that Ireland is safe; as to England there can be but little to dread, in my poor judgement, but from her connection with that troublesome Country. I hope the end of next month will quiet our minds on all that concerns home.

Elizabeth in Derbyshire was not without anxiety. In April 1798, in the last letter to her husband that has been preserved, she wrote:

Oh, my H., God grant they may give up the intended invasion. If not, how many brave Men shall we not have to lament, however short their stay.

For several months she had been worried by rumours of the alarming form that the invasion would take.

The French are more violent than ever in their Threats of invading us. Buonaparte is to command their Army (the Army of England). This day's Paper says " the following is handed about as the Plan which the Enemy have adopted for the purpose of invading this Country. . . . Thirty Rafts are to be built, they are to be composed of enormous quantities of Timber, connected in the strongest manner; they are to be provided with parapets of timber and Hides, cannon proof, with Artillery and furnaces to heat red hot balls; they are to be navigated with sails, Oars and rudders; each is to bring over 10,000 men, making in the whole 300,000. With a due proportion of horses and field Artillery they are to proceed from different ports of France, and to attempt a landing in different parts of this Island. Their red hot balls are to serve to repel the attack of a fleet of line of Battle Ships, while their own immersion will render them incombustible. Their small draft of Water will enable them to approach the flattest coast; their enormous bulk, covering a great number of Waves, will prevent their being much agitated by the motion of the Sea; and by means of Drawbridges affixed to them each raft will disgorge its myriad upon the English there ".

Truly there is no tale too wild to be believed in time of war; Elizabeth evidently had some slight doubts of this story, for she continued:

You, my H., will be the best judge of the practicability of this horrid plan. I think you will be surprised that they should thus openly prepare us for their approach, and will be a little incredulous; but so it is their schemes are discussed in the Convention.

The children at Dronfield were beginning to grow out of babyhood and, like most children of former days, they began their lessons at an early age. When he was 4 Charles was beginning to read.

My Charles (aged 5½) will be able very soon to write Papa a letter. If he begins early to write one line at a time, he will not suffer from confinement or the constrained attitude from which children at first, I am persuaded, suffer.

And six months later:

I do think my dear Charles almost longs to know how to write a letter to Papa. Might he begin to write a very little every day without confining him to it for more than half an hour at a time.

And again:

My sweet little Jane is, I am quite sure, as anxious to learn as her Brother. I quite long to hear her read.

The 6-year-old boy had been put into trousers for the first time and his proud mother had sent her husband a full description of Charles's appearance and his progress in learning.

Dronfield, 16 September 1797

Our dear Charles is become a very pretty Boy and more improved by his trousers than you can conceive. I first intended he should wear a Green Jacket with Nankeen Trousers like his Cousins; but Boy's dresses are made so short waisted that they will not look well. So since the hot weather began he has worn all Nankeen and his green Cloth is put by for the Winter, and he is the *prettiest made* gentlemanly little fellow you ever saw. His Clothes were beautifully made by a Man at Chesterfield; old Bounds has made a *second* Nankin very well by it. Dear Charles's hair does not curl tho' it cannot be called straight; but it is of little consequence at present for Gentlemen's Children are generally cropt. The dear Boy improves in his reading and understands what he reads. Mrs Barbauld's Hymns in Prose are intended to be committed to memory and recited. Last Monday Charles for the first time got two verses by heart in a short time.

He is much pleased with his employment and I think him very quick and he is very correct. You promised to write him a letter, my dear H., as soon as you heard he could read. Poor little Jane, she comes on by very slow degrees, but my patience with her Brother was so amply rewarded that I am not disheartened. I think she has improved within these two days and reads quite as well as Charles did at her age. Charles can almost say his Catechism, he has long read it through without mistake. I find that the best way of teaching him, and he has read the answers to my questions two or three times a week.

In August Charles wrote a letter with his own hand, which his father received in April 1798.

A glimpse of Elizabeth Harness, courageously carrying on her children's upbringing, is given in a small brown, leather-covered diary and account book for this year of 1797. Every week or two there is an entry " wrote to my dear Mr Harness " or " a letter from dear Mr Harness "—those letters which took so many months to arrive. Household matters and little acts of charity are faithfully recorded by the careful house-keeper (she was then about 32). A frequent entry is " Beggar ½d ", and from time to time a certain Molly Hawley is paid sums varying from 1s. to 5s. for " the poor children's school-ing ". Five times during the year occurs the " Great Wash " and on other occasions ale and small beer are brewed. Milk goes up 1d. a gallon, and the fact that the family had rabbits for dinner is worthy of mention. Sixpence is spent on sending Nanny to the Play and three days later the two maids go for 1s. An occasional 2d. is spent on toys. The children's doings are now and then reported. Jemima is inoculated, she has her first shoes, which cost 1s. 3d., and a little later on she walks alone. Jane is learning to sew and 1s. is spent on a thimble for her. A good deal of money, according to the standards of the time, is spent on clothes for Charles. " Cloth for Charles's night and day shirts " costs £1. 6s., cambric for Charles is 13s., the making of his clothes 12s. 6d., and blue cloth for his great-coat 14s. 6d. For herself Mrs Harness noted that 12s. 3d. is spent on " a straw bonnet lined ". Letters are a heavy expense and cost anything from 6d. to 1s. 6d. It is a quiet life that is thus chronicled. The chief excitement (apart from William's letters) is drinking tea with the neighbours. Aunt Croke is a frequent companion on these expeditions; and in turn the same friends come to drink tea and sometimes stay to supper.

A quiet life, but on the whole, apart from the constant pain of separation, a happy one. Elizabeth enjoyed her home, her simple social activities—" a rubber or two every evening " when she had visitors—her " dirty walks " in the country with Mrs Croke or a friend—often Mrs Biscoe—" assisted by a high pair of pattens ". Above all she enjoyed the children she was bringing up so carefully and well. In another old diary which had evidently been given to the children, is an entry in a childish hand, " Mrs Croke gives Charles Jane and Jemima 2s. 6d. every birthday what a good Aunty ".

The arrival of James Walch at Dronfield coincided with the time of Elizabeth's financial troubles. She had indeed made some small protest at the idea of being saddled with the care of another and older boy; but the poor child had been ship-wrecked on his way to this country—it was several months before his parents knew if he were alive; and when he arrived on her doorstep, a pathetic figure with hardly any clothes, Elizabeth took him to her heart.

Dronfield, 20 April 1798

This poor little Walch coming without Cloathes is an unexpected event; and God knows I want money. I have the pleasure to say he is well and very good and I do not think he has shed a tear since he has been in Dronfield. He goes regularly to school Morning and Afternoon. If he is to go to Litchfield it will be an unpleasant thing to take him away from poor little Taylor, yet if I do not find out anything by your letter I think I shall send him to board; but he must be cloathed from head to foot before he can go, and that, as I am situated, will take up some time. His shirts are making. I cut out half a dozen last week and of course have put them out to be made. Charles, dear Boy, must have a new coat this summer. The Taylor will measure and get the Cloth for both at the same time; so poor James thinks nothing of the delay, tho' the Cloaths he has are so coarse and fit him so ill that it hurts me to think of the good things he has lost; and his good looks depend much upon his dress.

Charles, who was a year or two younger than James Walch, had also begun going to the school kept by " poor Mr Taylor ", but only for a short time each day.

My sweet Charles began writing the Monday after James arrived. They went to school together. I sent for him in an hour. I have done the same every day since. He is very attentive I find and does not blot his book. It is certainly better than having the Man at home; it gives him an idea of school *discipline* and from always being sent for in proper time he learns nothing wrong from mixing with the boys out of school hours.

In the same letter there is news of the little girls. Jane, " a dear engaging girl ", had not been well, but

Our little Fairy Jemima is quite well and as wild as possible. How you will love her. My Aunt Croke has long been very uneasy that poor dear Jemima has not been received into the Church. You know Mrs Parker and Aunt C. are [to be] her god-mothers. I am not less uneasy yet I felt so uncomfortable at your absence when dear Jane was Christened that I had not spirits even to do *my duty*, which it certainly is.

All was now arranged for the christening and Jemima's parent felt some not unnatural anxiety about the 2-year-old's be-haviour.

Poor little Soul, she is constantly talking of going to Church. I know not what she will say at the Font. I wish it was over. Oh my beloved friend, would to God you could be here.

In Ceylon Colonel Harness was beginning to think seriously about his son's education.

27 September 1798

Our Charles will be nearly seven years old by the time you receive this. What pleasure I promised myself in making easy to him the first Rudiments of his Latin, and introducing to him those real friends that will afford him pleasure and in-struction through life, the Classics. No body will take the pains that to his Father would have been delights. The time draws near when he should begin upon the troublesome part of his education, storing his memory with rules that, as his judgment expands, he will apply and have at hand. I wish a clever person could be found to come two hours in the day, which at first would be enough. He would certainly be better with such a mama for a year longer, and surely fate will not separate us longer. There is my little Jane too growing a good tall girl. I shall not know her; and mama will have taught her to read so well that I shall be quite charmed to hear her. My little Bessy will only have heard of her Papa.

The 7-year-old Charles, we learn from his mother " can learn his Hymns in the midst of bustle, for it sometimes happens that the Maids are engaged and cannot take the little saucy, chattering, *sensible* Bessy ". Miss Stephens had sent " a charm-ing collection of useful books " on grammar and geography and Charles " searches for every place we read of in the Map ". There is a pretty domestic picture of the boy and Aunt Croke " reading a clever little History of England, Mrs Trimmer's, James and Jane sitting by and little Jemima very still in the room ".

One cannot avoid a certain sympathy with the small boy, concentrating on his lessons " in the midst of bustle " and " storing his memory with rules ". By February 1799 his fond father was suggesting plans for more definite schooling.

My Charles will have gotten well into his eighth year before my own wife receives this letter. The period advances when he should be placed in a good School. My Bessy, this is a subject I see the importance of. It occupyes much of my serious attention; at the same time the distance that divides us leaves me without the power of consulting with you. On no account could I think he should be sent to a distance that would exclude him from passing his holidays at both vacations with the most affectionate of mothers. Find out the situation for him where his Education, health and morals, as well as manners, will be best secured, and place him in it with as little delay as may be necessary. Our dear Jane is under my Bessy's eye and for some time can want nothing.

In January 1799 the Colonel had somewhat changed his views on Indian affairs.

At Madras all wears the appearance of War. I am told the object is to strip Tippoo of his maritime Provinces so as to cut him off from European Allies. The Madras Government made a requisition for the 29th and 80th Regiments, but Mr North [1] refused it on the score of the Garrison in Ceylon being too weak.

Colonel Harness had no particular desire to leave Ceylon for the coast of India; but his orders to quit the island came eventually in a gratifying form.

---

[1] Frederick North, later 5th Earl of Guilford. He was Governor of Ceylon from 1798 to 1803. He initiated several reforms and *The Dictionary of National Biography* speaks of his " humane and beneficent sway ", in contrast to the behaviour of the former Dutch rulers.

Trincomallie, 22 February 1799

I was last evening most happily surprized by the receipt of the Letter I hasten to copy.

Calcutta, 25 January 1799

SIR,

I am directed by the Commander in Chief to acquaint you that in compliance with your wishes expressed to him in your letter of the 31st October 1798 he has taken the earliest opportunity in his power of promoting you to a Lieut. Colonelcy in the line, by appointing you to the 74th Regt in succession to Lieut Colonel Shaw who has been removed to the 12th Foot, which Sir Alured Clarke hopes will meet with your intire approbation.

I have the honor to be
    Sir
        Your most obedient
            Humble Servant
                WALTER CLIFFE
                    Adjt General

Nothing, my adored Bessy, would be more agreable to me than this promotion given in so flattering a way. The 74th is one of the first Regiments to leave India and it would not at all surprize me, should that happy period be not protracted by unforeseen events, that I should fold my own Bessy to my heart before the expiration of the year. I mean to leave this place as soon as I can, in a few days. The Regiment is in the neighbourhood of Madras. I am told a very gentlemanly Corps.

The 74th was a Scottish regiment, now represented by the Highland Light Infantry. The new command therefore involved considerable change of uniform. " For the first time I shall mount the thistle. The kilt and the Philybag will be also new." It was therefore as a Highlander that Colonel Harness embarked upon the next period of his service abroad.

8

Disappointment in India

COLONEL HARNESS was at Madras waiting to join his new regiment when the British resumed hostilities against Tippoo Sultan. In March 1799 that troublesome person was shut up in his capital, Seringapatam.

> Madras, 13 April 1799
>
> I waited yesterday the fleet coming to anchor and am rewarded with your dear letter of the 13th August. I shall join you before the expiration of the year. I am now on my way, having waited a month at this place, to join my Regiment. They are with the army before Seringapatem, which it is fairly presumed has surrendered. Tippoo has been taken at unawares, he recedes before a handful of men. I go to waite at Kistnagherry the return of the army. My Baggage went off two days ago and I follow in my Palankeen this evening. The chief reason of the Reinforcements which are sent out is the discontent which was lately manifested by the Company's European Troops; it has therefore been considered advisable to reform them and send the King's Troops in their stead.

William Harness was a little previous in his guessing. It was not until 4 May that Seringapatam was finally captured and the evil, fanatical Tippoo slain. The 74th were present at the storming of the capital, though their newly appointed Colonel had not as yet been able to join them. By 16th May he was with his new regiment.

> Seringapatnam
>
> You will read the place from whence this letter comes to you, as I do, with wonder. On my reaching Kistnagherry I found Col. Read was within three days march, proceeding

up the Ghauts,[1] where he was to fall in with Genl Floyd's detachment to escort him to the army. I of course did not delay an instant to get up with him and had the good fortune to reach Genl F. on the 26th of April. We learnt on the 6th Inst. that the Sultan had been killed and this important Capital had been stormed on the 4th. The 74th has suffered in Officers; but the prize articles and plunder is immense. Large Ingots of Gold have been sold by the Soldiers for ten Pagodas and very valuable Jewels for a Bottle of Brandy. In walking round the Fort my amazement is at every step heightened at the possibility of a Fortress of such strength, defended by half an Empire, falling before the courage and conduct of a handful of determined Men. The carnage of a sacked capital may be imagined. Thousands threw themselves over the ramparts into the Cauvery. Its rapid stream is infected for miles. Col. Wellesley is put into the place; while calling on him the day after I arrived, the provost reported to him that he had buryed nine thousand and the works are far from being cleared. It appears that the attack was made at a most critical moment, that all the provisions were exhausted and that the Troops that led the Storm went absolutely fasting. The Town was richly stored. The money and Jewels that are now sealed by the Prize Agents exceeds a million Sterling. There is a large room full of Boxes of Jewels which are not yet examined. There are every day sales of Trinkets mostly French, but much as I wished to procure a few for presents at home, they go at so enormous a rate that no prudence can authorize the purchase, particularly as it is not a decided point whether I am entitled to share with the Captors. Should I be so fortunate, and I have Genl Harris to side with me, I hope it will be, my adored wife, something to ensure an easy oeconomical independence for our lives, that I shall return to you with five thousand pounds including my savings in Ceylon, which with my Commission and the wreck of our former fortune will render us very comfortable. This unexpected attack on Tippoo has deferred our embarkation for which the order had been issued. It may require some months to settle a captive Kingdom but all the surviving chief's and Tippoo's Sons are already come in. The Bombay army and the Nizam's con-

[1] *Ghaut*—a pass or defile.

Indian military scenes after drawings by Henry Alkan.

(*Reproduced by kind permission of Messrs George Newnes Ltd.*)

The "clumsy" silver bird from Tippoo's palace.

tingent have already moved off. Should I fortunately be considered a sharer how lucky will this remove to the 74th prove to me.

He goes on to speak of Tippoo's scorched earth policy.

In my long march through Tippoo's dominions not a single house was left standing. He had done much by way of distressing us for forage &c, but whatever he had spared was plundered and burnt by the Nizamites. All round Seringapatnam the same devastation prevails; the Town without the Fort is a heap of ruins, the Palaces have received little injury. They disappointed the ideas I had formed of the residence of an Eastern Sultan. The Tomb of Hyder is the most magnificent thing on the Island.[1] The whole is formed for the Tyrant ruler. His Palaces, Zananas, gardens are but kept up and protected by all the rest; for him all is formed, for his Subjects nothing. Their habitations, the best of them, would be miserable cottages in England. All is now ruin and confusion.

The heat on the pass ascending the Ghauts was greater than I had ever experienced, beyond all calculation, within the tents the Thermometer stood at 125 degrees: in the sun one was placed but it mounted so rapidly that the owner ordered it under cover, fearing it would burst. I suffered much from restlessness, but in health I am under the protection of Heaven for the greater the change the greater force and stock of health do I feel to possess. I had the happiness to join this Corps after a march in the most sultry season, through a Country perfectly unknown and not laid down even in the topical maps, in the best health. I saw so little to oppose and felt so much security that I did not load my Pistols till I reached Col. Read's Division, when I had travelled about two hundred miles through the Enemy's Country. The Officers are a very Gentlemanly set of Men and the Regiment bears a high character in India.

The next letter tells of disappointment.

[1] Seringapatam lies on an island in the River Canvery.

Camp near Seringapatem, 9 June 1799

I am told a ship will leave Madras in about a fortnight. You perhaps will have received my other letter with the good news of the Capture of this whole country. It was all so good that it is painful to contradict any part of it, particularly what so nearly concerns ourselves. I am sorry to find I am not to be included among the Sharers of the Prize Money. The Committee have excluded every Body who did not actually serve at the seige. Having had my hopes raised to so high a pitch by what I considered authority, by the Commander in Chief's order and the usages of all former times I feel my disappointment very great. The prize property too turns out much greater than was supposed—a Lieut. Colonel will get in the first payment immediately to be paid two thousand Pounds, and the second division it is judged will considerable exceed the first. I find too the stay of the Regiment in India is protracted but I trust not for a long time. New Regiments are every day coming out and as soon as this country is settled some must return to Europe and we are the first. Many of the Officers under this impression are making exchanges into Regiments that have lately come out. I must confess I write more out of spirits than I have long done but why did I suffer them to be so immoderately raised? The national advantages are great. If I had arrived in time, and I was only prevented by waiting on the Ghouts for Col. Brown's Detachment (who is to be brought to an account for his delay), I should have had the honor of commanding His Majesty's 74th Regiment at the storm. It is painful, doubly painful, to waite here spending my best years if it is not to be to the advantage of my family—but it is supposed Col. Campbell will exchange which will be a very great advantage, and even this delay may prevent my being reduced to the halfpay. In short, my adored wife, Heaven has ever been peculiarly indulgent in the blessings I enjoy and it is impious to repine. My sweet children I shall see in a year I trust at the very farthest. I have given none of the news of this place—it is little interesting. The Army is kept hovering about the Capital to keep all quiet till a Government is formed. The Throne is broken to pieces, the poor sons saw it in pieces. Tippoo had never ascended. As he approached it he caught the eye of the Tiger that supported it, and a superstitious idea coming across his mind he said he would waite till the present troubles were over. It was very rich. Thank God I have made no purchases of the very tempting things that exceeded calculation. Col. Wallace is a very estimable man and much esteemed: the only unpleasant thing I feel in coming to the 74th is being put over him, his pretentions were so honourable. He commanded the first division of the Regt on its raising and brought it out. He has been three times at Seringapatem and commanded the Grenadiers at the storming the Pettah by Lord Cornwallis. His conduct in the present war has been eminently conspicuous. He is particularly noted in the thoughts of the Commander in Chief. Col. Campbell did wonders, but losing his Boots in crossing the river in a previous attack, he was lamed by the sharp rocks and was incapable of leading the Regt at the assault.

The instances of generosity among the Soldiers are creditable to humanity. Their first object was to go to the Hospital and distribute to every sick man. One poor fellow complainted that he was very ill and had had no sleep for two nights. " Then Tom there is a pillow shall make you sleep ", was the answer while his comrade tucked a bag with two hundred pagodas under his head. An Officer saw a good man give away handfuls of untold gold to a worthless fellow and remonstrated on his dividing his money with such a character. " Ah Sir, he has always been an unlucky Dog to himself but a very good Comrade to me—he once saved my life "—but instances are numberless. A fellow who had been employed as a Butcher in his company has given away his cash by the hundreds " but for all this ", he says, " you shall pay me for the couple of Beef Steaks, for that is a just debt ". But alas, with much real charitable affection there is full as much disregard of Money as the Navy even can produce. A Soldier urges in his defence, when tried for Drunkenness on Duty, that he could not resist the temptation, having been able to get a few drams at a Crown apiece. The common prize given for a bottle of spirits was twelve Pagodas or four pounds sixteen shillings. A Soldier is purchasing a Company for his Lieutenant. This part of India at this season is so cold that I feel not to have sufficient covering with a very thick Blanket and

Counterpane. I see by this morning's State we have but twelve sick. The wounded were left at Seringapatem. We are now about fifteen miles from it. We can ride all day. The Sun is warm but there is always a comfortable breeze. If all India was like this I should beg you to come to me and make up my mind to remain several years; but all my wishes desires and thoughts are *home*.

As Colonel Harness had foreseen, the attack on Tippoo, successful as it was, delayed for several months the regiment's return to England. On 22 June a treaty was signed for the partition of Mysore. The Nizam of Hyderabad, the East India Company and the Mahrattas were all allotted a share. But here already was the beginning of further trouble. The Mahrattas, recently, with the Nizam, our somewhat uncertain allies in the struggle against Tippoo, moved by jealousy and unfriendly feeling towards the English, refused to accept their not very large share of the partitioned state. A threatening question was beginning to arise—a question about which there would surely at that time be no doubt felt in English breasts. Who would wield the mastery in India? Would it be England or the Mahratta chiefs or—a sinister, distant shadow— Napoleon and France? A desperate struggle was yet to come.

On 27 July William Harness wrote, cheerfully enough on the whole, from camp near Chitteldroog:

This place is about a hundred and fifty miles from Seringa- patnam, one of the strongest Forts in India; like every other in Mysore, since the surrender of the Capital, it has submitted without a shot. We have been marching almost without intermission through an uncultivated but, for want of In- habitant, very productive soil, like a park run to ruins, but with large herds of antelopes. The climate is very temperate, so much so as to render exercise in the Sun even pleasant during the whole of the day. The happy termination of the Indian War will I hope hasten our departure. A few days ago I sat next to Genl Harris at dinner. He expected the order to send the Regiment home by the next Fleet. I fear the General is too sanguine, for until Buonoparte is disposed of I fear no orders will arrive for Troops leaving this Country.

I have just read the last news from England dated March. The war appeared far from being at an end. Ireland presents but a cloudy sky. In every other quarter the prospect brightens, but while I write a crisis surely must be approaching; what a bloody close to the century.

In October there was the first mention of further trouble with the followers of Tippoo Sultan.

Camp, 5 October 1799

You will wish to know where the indefinite date of this letter would say that I am. We are, my Bessy, on the Banks of the Wordah which borders the Soondah Country and separates the dominions of the late Sultan from the Maratta Frontier. At the capture of Seringapatnam a Prisoner was liberated from his Dungeon and his Irons, who immediately found means from the wreck of Tippoo's army to assemble a force sufficient to waste all on his route, and, like a snowball gathering as he went, (for all the discontented fled to him) he became so formidable as to require the whole of this army to drive him out of the conquered country. He has been repeatedly defeated and his followers scattered in every direction but in a few days has reappeared in increased force. He is now completely driven from the Country and has taken refuge with the Marattas, a small tribe of which he has joined himself to, and we have just heard has defeated the army of Pursemen Bow,[1] the most warlike and powerful of the confederated alliance, having taken him at unawares. As the whole of the Mysore Country is now considered as secured, Colonel Wellesley with Purniah (Tippoo's prime minister) are gone into the Soondah Country to settle the posts. Colonel Campbell accompanys him, so that the command of the Army devolved on me. This is the 10th day of their absence.

While I have been writing Major Macauley (our Resident in Mysore) has just called to say an Hyrcarnah[2] is arrived from the Bow. He has brought the most beautiful Shawls he had

[1] This is almost certainly Paraśuramā Bhāū (according to the Librarian of the India Office Library), one of the leaders of the Marāthā army in the Mysore wars against Haidar Alī and Tipū Sultan. He was killed in 1799. Bhāū means literally " brother ", but is frequently used as an honorific ending to personal names.

[2] *Hyrcarrah*, an Anglo-Indian term for a courier, a spy, or a messenger.

139

ever seen. They are directed for Genl Harris or Officer Commanding but he says I must avoid Colonel Wellesley seeing them as they being offered officially and refused would be considered as an affront.

This is a beautiful Country, rich to luxuriancy, but almost without Inhabitants having been in '71 completely desolated.

(Later.) Accounts are just brought in of the Bow being killed. He was our strong Maratta ally during my Lord Cornwallis's campaignes. I am glad to find the Marattas are so weak, exhausted and divided as to have nothing to apprehend from that quarter for many years. Anxious as I am for home you will not wonder at my calculating every contingency which might even remotely tend to detain us here. There are at present twenty King's Regts in India with every Enemy subdued; while the implacable Tippoo lived the establishment never exceeded ten.

My little Jane will I hope have my comfortable stockings ready. How I long to see her work. Our little Bessy must have strange ideas of a papa.

It must have been shortly after writing this letter that William Harness received some directions from Colonel Wellesley.

On the Public Service,
Soopah, 4 October 1799

Sir

I have the pleasure to inform you that I took possession of the Fort of Soopah yesterday without opposition. The Peons of the Rajah of Soondah of which there had been a number in the Fort quitted it on the day before when they heard of the Action with the Mahrattahs at Sambranee. The people complain that they have been plundered, but the Soondah Rajah has not had time to drive off the Inhabitants as he and the Mahrattahs had in other parts of the province.

I shall leave here either one or two Companies of the 1st of the 1st according as I shall find that there are certain Means of Subsistence for them. As however I have found the utmost difficulty in procuring Subsistence for the Troops (even for my own small escort) I have determined to secure it in some degree as well against the Consequences of what the Mah-rattas and other Plunderers have done as against what they may do hereafter when the army is withdrawn, by sending into Soondah and distributing in the different posts which I intend should be occupied a large proportion of the Grain at present in charge of the Grain Depmt. I therefore request that as soon as you receive this Letter you will send across the Werdah to Mundnagoor under a sufficient escort six Hundred Loads of that Rice. I shall send orders to Mundnagoor for its distribution. If Captain Macfarlane and his Battallion should not have crossed the Werdah when you will receive this Letter it will be advisable to send the Grain with him.

The 1st of the 1st is very deficient in Musquet Ammunition and it is very desirable that some should be sent forward and you will be so kind as to send a proportion of that in Camp in charge of the same escort.

As it appears that the Troops at present in Soondah are sufficient to settle it and as the loss which the Mahrattahs sustained in the Action at Samaranee makes it probable that they will not enter the Country again, I have determined to place the Army farther back, with a view to their being nearer their supplies, and to being clear of the Rains. As soon as convenient after you will receive this Letter you will move by easy Marches to Shikarpour where you will be so kind as to remain till you hear further from me. I shall order the Native Cavalry to join you as soon as I hear that Captain Macfarlane's Battalion is across the Werdah.

I shall set out on my return to the Army to-morrow and shall proceed by Soondah.

I have the Honor to be

Sir

Your Obed^t Servt

Arthur Wellesley

If any musquet ammunition should have been sent into Soondah in consequence of my letter to Major Macauley of the 29th Sepr You need not send any more.

There is no record in the Colonel's letters of the carrying out of these directions and we hear of him next at Bangalore. Young Charles's education was progressing: " I am delighted

141

with my dear Boy's Letters and shall talk French with him all day." Often the fond father mentions that he has written to his son, but only one of these letters remains. It is a long letter and gives the further story of the elusive Doondia, the liberated prisoner. The chase after this resourceful brigand occupied many weary, adventurous weeks. It was not until 10 September that Colonel Wellesley, who had pursued him into the Mahratta country, was able to overtake and finally overpower him. Colonel Harness had evidently borne his part in the first stage of this stern pursuit.

Palace of Bangalore,
16 January 1800

My very dear Boy,

Your two letters have both given me very great pleasure and I thank you for them. I do not know how to tell you how very happy they made me, but you will be able partly to guess when you recollect that you talk in them of your Mama, your Sisters, Aunty and yourself, and that I love you all better than anybody else in this whole world so that to see your very names written is a pleasure; but to be told that you are happy and think of and love me, as I read in your letters, and when we are so far from each other, is a happiness I can only enjoy in reading your letters and your dear Mama's. I wish my Charles very much to see you and hope in a very few months my Regiment will be ordered to go to England, but as you know that does not depend upon me. We expected to come home very soon after Tippoo Sultaun was killed, and his family made prisoners; but he was a cruel man and the English, who shudder to hear of cruel things, when they got possession of his Capital were very glad to release all the prisoners that they found shut up in dungeons with heavy irons on them, and almost starving to death.

There were a great many that his cruel man had confined, not as in England because they were bad and wicked men, but because he did not like them. These poor men were all delighted to see their families and to gain their liberty; but one man, who had used when a boy to carry the Sultaun's slippers, and had learnt to be as wicked as himself, had no sooner got the irons knocked off his hands and legs than he began to rob and to persuade Tippoo's Soldiers, the worst of them, to join with him, and as they had no body to pay them several thousand entered and served under Doondiah which is the name of the ci-devant Slipper-carrier. They set out in a large body and set fire to every village they came to, took away all the money in it, and all the horses and cattle and forced away with them all the men. If they met with any opposition they killed all the old men, and all the women and children, in a way that it would almost make you cry to read. He then became so strong, for he had forced so many people to serve him, had stolen so much money, and he had taken several Forts with a great many cannon in them and guns, that General Harris was obliged to follow him with a numerous army. You will be surprised to hear that some very good men, who had a great deal of money and kept several thousand Soldiers, should join themselves to this wicked, ungrateful man; but they were faithful to their old master and King, and could not forgive the English for killing him, although you know it was his own fault to make the war. These people knew all the strong places in the country and all the roads, and travelled so secretly that we could not sometimes tell whereabouts they were; for they would sometimes separate and go in small parties and, as they were dressed like the country people, we did not know them; so that we marched many hundred miles at one time, hearing of Towns being burnt by him in one place, at other times cruelties committed in others. However Colonel Dalrymple, who speaks this country language, was sent forward with the Cavalry and he marched all night and in the morning came up with him and his Army at breakfast, when the Cavalry fell upon them and killed several hundred of them. After this Colonel Dalrymple had people to tell whichever way he went, and after pursuing him over rivers, very broad and rapid, for several months, and killing a great many of his people, he was completely driven out of the country; and when the country people saw we took their parts and paid for everything we had and used them much better than their former King, they began to be happy and to return to their homes. But travelling so far, in many places where there are no roads, and in this very hot country has been very fatiguing.

Our Baggage was carryed on Elephants, Camels, Mules and Oxen and on men and women's heads. An army in India on the march has a very odd look. The Elephants are very useful creatures. I had always one to carry my tent. I used to like to see it lay down to be loaded and to have its load taken off, and see it bend its leg for its keeper to stand upon and then raise him upon it until he mounted him. They are very good-natured animals and, as you have been told, very sagacious. My keeper used to set down his child who was about three years old between the Elephant's forelegs, and trunk, and put him in his charge. The child would try to get away but the Elephant would, after he had got a few yards, put his trunk round him and place him again in his seat. He was an Elephant nurse. We had no bridges across any of the rivers and over some the whole army crossed on Elephants' backs. Six men rode at a time with their arms and knapsacks. It appeared to me, when the Elephant stood up, that he was mounting into the air. The motion is not unpleasant, and they are so careful to feel their way as they go along and so wise as never to attempt what they are unequal to, that it is the safest way of travelling in the world. The Black men of Ronta [1] travel on them in great state. They have a kind of house they call a Howda which holds four people with seats and pillows, made very comfortable, in which they sit and play chess when they please. I intended to write about several things that would amuse you when I sat down, but this nasty Doondiah has taken up so much of my paper that I must reserve them for my next letter. I am living in a very splendid palace of the Sultaun's.

Tell my Jane that I long to see a letter from her, and tell Jemina too that she has made me very happy by giving me a lock of her hair, and tell Aunty Croke to wear her shawl whenever the weather is cold enough, and tell your dear Mama that one of the happiest hours in my life will be that when I can see her and our dear Children in health. What a happy family we shall be! Adieu! my dear Boy. What a pleasure to have a good boy for my own son. You will always make your Mama and I very happy because you will always be very good. I have not said one word of your French, much as I like to hear people speak French. I think people are more civil to each

---

[1] I have been unable to identify this name. *C.M.D.-J.*

other in speaking French than even in speaking our own language. Again my dear Charles adieu! I write because I am unwilling to stop but I hope my letter will not be too late.

I am, my Charles,
Your very affectionate Father
William Harness

The New Year had opened happily with a renewed prospect of receiving the prize money.

This is said to be an eventful country; sure the Globe does not possess another to match it. Could I have supposed we could be detained here till the commencement of another year, which I am witnessing? And after giving up all for lost, could I foresee my Lord Mornington would reverse all plans and give me a share in the prize, which I learn from the best authority to be actually the case? My first dividend will be from six to seven thousand pagodas. My Angel, with what delight shall I put it into your lap.

Another letter, written that same January 1800, dated the 15th, from the Palace of Bangalore, confirmed this happy prospect, and it was " with a pleasure of the first water " that he wrote to Elizabeth that all would be well. " This has been a subject of great anxiety to me. It is a long story that will amuse us on a winter's evening now it has so happily terminated." So far, so good; but the quest of the elusive prize money, which was to relieve the family of all further financial anxiety, continued for more than three years. It delayed, and finally prevented the Colonel's return home. That William Harness's desire to return to England was not looked upon without sympathy by a higher authority is shown by this kindly letter from Colonel Wellesley.

Seringapatam, 2 February 1800
My dear Colonel,
I have received your letter of the 31st January which has given me great satisfaction. It rarely happens (particularly in this country) that it is in the power of an officer in command to please those who are under his orders; and when he is so

fortunate it is to be attributed as much to their good dispositions as to any efforts he may have made for that purpose. I regret exceedingly on publick as well as on private grounds, that the 74 rgt. is removed from Bangalore; But you must have been long enough in this country to perceive that the public Interest and convenience are not upon all occasions the cause of the publick measures.

I don't think that your corps will be drafted. At least not for some time; although I have seen the resolutions of thanks from the Court of Directors, and their songs of triumph, the best Item of all of which is the prospect of permanent peace in India, and of course the consequent diminution of the military establishments and expences.

I think you are right in going to England even if the 74th should remain here.

Believe me, My Dear Colonel
Yours most faithfully,
Arthur Wellesley

Lieut.-Col. Harness,
  74th rgt.

William's letter from Bangalore Palace continues:

My health has borne the fatigues of this Campaign under the torrid zone with as little injury as it underwent during the frosts in Germany. I have marched at the least fifteen hundred miles since I left Trincomallie. The heat was almost intolerable. The Command of the army devolved on me for more than a month on the Maratta Boundaries. Col. Wellesley had left us to settle districts where no line of demarkation had been determined. We have been in this place since the first of December.

In the field the bare wages of my servants costs me above five hundred pounds a year. I was living with men whose pockets were all over flowing with prize money, and of course every thing was at an exorbitant price. I found an income of good twelve hundred pounds a year too little. During Wellesley's absence I had the Staff of the Army to feed. In short I was growing unhappy. I was growing in debt in India while my adored wife was in want at home, and such was the situation that it must have been supported. I was nine months in the field traversing a Country a very large portion of which had never been trodden by Europeans.

A Mr Clarke has just given us divine service, the first I have been able to attend in India. He is a Buckinghamshire man from the neighbourhood of Newport Pagnal. He was delighted to perform the first Christian rites in the palace of the Sultaun.

I am living in a splendid palace and occupy a large pavillion of it. The arcade where I write is six and thirty feet long with two rows of beautifully painted and gilt pillars. The front verandah is upwards of fifty feet, there are three rooms on each hand besides offices; the door frames are all gilt as are all the cornices.

The King's Speech had evidently caused some heartburning among his soldiers in India:

The Post has just brought us the King's Speech on the 24th September, and an account of the action of the 19th of that month. Expectation is all alive for the sequel. The Battle of Novi [1] must have prevented the army of Holland being re-inforced to a very great extent. We were surprized to find so little mention made of the conquest of this immense Empire.

In February 1800 the regiment was on the march for Trichinipoly. " The prize money is not yet paid. The Jewels are put into a Lottery "; and William Harness had purchased a lottery ticket for his Bessy. At Trichinopoly he was again magnificently lodged.

I found Zamor here, I had not seen him for nearly a year. He could not have gone through the campagne, and I left him at Madras. He has brought me a little furniture to my large house. You will suppose it large when I tell you one of my rooms is eighty feet long. I had the whole detachment at Church in it last Sunday.

[1] Novi Ligure in Piedmont, scene of a victory by the Austrians and Russians over the French in 1799.

Until now William Harness had been exceedingly happy in his new regiment, that " very gentlemanly corps ". " Colonel Campbell and I ", he wrote, " hit it off admirably well, he is uncommonly civil and well bred. The whole business of the Regiment he leaves to me." In April, however, a grim cloud appeared on the horizon. In a short, agitated note he wrote:

I have been writing a long letter to the Duke of York and another to Colonel Brownrigg for I have just learnt that my appointment to the 74th Regiment is not approved of at home. This is very painful to me; however it makes me the more anxious to get home. I cannot return to the 80th as Major after commanding the Army in the Field for above a month, and the European Brigade for a considerable time, and serving so successfully for fifteen months as the Lt. Colonel of a Regiment. I have explained all this as forcibly as I could.

This honourable record of service with the 74th was " forcibly " though restrainedly pointed out in his letter to the Duke, in which he appealed to the royal Commander-in-Chief's understanding of the mind of a soldier.

12 April 1800

Your Royal Highness is too well acquainted with a Soldier's feelings and what they ought to be not to conceive, after serving so successfully for fifteen months as the Lt Colonel of a Regiment, the pain I must suffer in returning to do the duty of Major with two Lieut. Colonels over me. I served as the senior Major on the Continent in the winter Campaign of 95, at the capture of the Soldanah Fleet in 96 and have never been absent from my Regiment during the whole War. Perhaps this is the only situation that can excuse a man talking of himself, but to apologize to your Royal Highness were unnecessary for a Soldier's laying before his Commander in Chief his services and to solicit his protection with the profoundest respect and every consideration.

In spite of its conventional expression it was a moving appeal, but it apparently met with no response. This uncertainty was to be a harassing cause of anxiety for some months to come.

His worries were increased by receiving in May letters telling more of the difficulties in which Elizabeth found herself through their agent's financial failure.

>   Trichinopoly, 24 May 1800
> I am, my dearest wife, in the most uncomfortable state. I told you in my last it was reported here that the Duke of York had not confirmed the promotions but had appointed Col. Harcourt to the 12th as soon as he had seen Col. Acton's death and before he had seen Sir Alured Clarke's arrangement. Sir Alured thinks he will do it away and waites for further information. In the mean time it is very uncomfortable. I am ordered with the 74th to Bangalore, it will take a month to march there. At Bangalore I think it very likely I shall receive the order to rejoin the 80th. This suspense is the more uncomfortable as it prevents my being able to ask leave; however I trust time will be given me before October. Good God, my Bessy, who could have believed when I was appointed to the 74th the Regiment would have remained here till this time.

He explains the likelihood of still further delay and presents a somewhat uncomfortable picture:

> The extent of Country acquired by the late War makes more troops necessary than are in the Country; for at a distance from the Garrison discontented Spirits will ever arise, refuse to pay their Khist [1] and require Troops to quiet them, on the approach of which they disperse and are not heard of untill the troops are again at a distance. This has ever been the case in India, but it may now be fairly supposed to increase since the territory is so widely increased, and the army not augmented. The 12th Regiment and Colonel Shawe with it is gone into the Nizam's Country where we have already a strong force. The Nizam is turned eighty and it is important to the Company that his Succession should be in its interests. It is said he and the Company are for appointing the eldest son, but that there are interests in favor of the 2nd, on the

---

[1] " *Kist*. An instalment of the yearly land revenue or other payment." (*Oxford English Dictionary*.)

score of the incapacity of his brother. The British force is likely to turn the scale. This is said to give cause of umbrage to the Marattas who have not shewn themselves neighbourly since we have begun to elbow them so closely—but they are poor and disunited.

By the end of August the matter was decided. Colonel Harness was to return to the 80th Regiment—a return that was made doubly bitter, not only by the loss of command but by the unfriendly reception accorded him by its Colonel. He had now been a year and half in command of the 74th, had seen much gruelling service with the Scottish Regiment, had been a successful and conscientious commanding officer; yet such was the lack of cohesion between the authorities in England and the Commander-in-Chief in India that his appointment by Sir Alured Clarke was never acknowledged and in the official record of his service there is no mention of his ever having left the 80th.[1] On the ever present question of leave for an early return to England Colonel Champagné appears to have been, to say the least, obstructive. On 26 August William Harness was staying with his good friend, General Bridges.

General Bridges, with whom I am, is a very aimable man, he has a large fortune. Mrs B. has a house in Baker Street and lives in a handsome style. He expects Lady Clive [2] here in a few days with her two daughters. This is the scene where the Lord Clive first displayed those talents that acquired his endless name. The Girls have been reading Orme's history and are impatient to mark the spots he had celebrated. The whole plain here is marked with his victories, we are brushing up our localities to be on a par.

General Bridges and I drive out in his curricle every evening, we are forming plans all the way. His immense fortune allows

[1] The Chief Library Clerk of the Royal United Service Institution points out that Colonel Harness " was not gazetted to the 74th Foot ", and that had his apointment been approved " he would certainly have had his name gazetted in the London Gazette ", and that therefore he was only attached to the 74th.

[2] Wife of the 2nd Lord Clive (afterwards Earl of Powis) who was Governor of Madras from 1798 to 1803.

him to indulge every wish, and so does my small one, for I have no ambition to be great. We must be respectable and we are happy; and at ease we shall be when this separation is past.

He had not forgotten the Dronfield cellar for he added: I have had a pipe of Madeira for this year past in the store at Madras to bring home with me, it will not suffer by remaining.

This wine, however, did not find its way to Dronfield, but was sent as a present to the Colonel's old and good friend, Lord Harrington.

20 September 1800

Colonel Champagné has written to me to join, and I am preparing for Trincomallie. He is very inconsiderate, not to say unfeeling, unfriendly and cruel. I was sitting next Lady Clive at Supper when I received his Letter, and I put it into her hand. She had been giving me commissions for home. There is not occasion for three Field Officers being with the Regiment, and were I to make a public application to the Commander in Chief I should not be refused, but I cannot do this without quarrelling with Champagné and I would avoid it if possible. General Bridges kindly says " tell Mrs Harness it is not I that detains you ". Zamor and my Baggage leave this house in the morning and I follow in two days. If I had left this aimable friendly man, even to have gone home, I should not have parted with him without regret.

With his usual resilience William Harness discovered some consolation for the further delay in the fact that the prize money had not yet been paid and that it would have been unwise to have left for home without it. He reflected that " I have very frequently found the failure of my very best wishes attended with future advantage."

January 1801 found him once more at Trincomali. He found the place much improved, " the underwood cut down and every body in high health ".

Governor North has been here. He is very witty, abounds in anecdote and without any affectation. He did me the favor to dine with me. Colonel Champagné has asked and obtained leave for himself to proceed to Europe but I am persuaded he does not mean to avail himself of it. His fondness for money has so far the ascendancy over every passion and consideration, that I cannot bring myself to believe he thinks seriously of leaving India. I look upon Sir Alured Clarke's leaving India as very ill timed for my interests; he has written to tell me he was greatly mortifyed at my promotion not being confirmed at home through the previous appointment of Colonel Harcourt.

Young Charles's future education occupied more and more of his father's thoughts. The pros and cons of obtaining a commission in the army for this small boy were constantly and carefully weighed. The project had been mooted years before when Colonel Harness was in the Low Countries, but it was never brought to a conclusion. Now the commission was to become an accomplished fact and in a particularly gracious form. Did the Commander-in-Chief, who always regarded William Harness with warm friendship, perhaps wish to atone to him in some measure for the bitter disappointment over the command of the 74th?

25 January 1801

Sir Alured Clarke has given Charles an Ensigncy. If it can be avoided I should not like him to know it. Conceive my surprize at receiving the letter, of which the following is an extract, from the Adjutant General. " I have the pleasure to inform you, by desire of Sir Alured Clarke, that he has nominated your Son, Mr Harness, to an Ensigncy without purchase in the 80th Regiment. Sir William Clarke solicited the Commander in chief the 84th Regiment when an opportunity should offer to do so, but as that is not likely to occur during the General's stay in India, and conceiving it would be more desirable to you to have your son in the Regiment with yourself, Sir Alured Clarke has much satisfaction in availing himself of the occasion that has now offered to do what he hopes will be gratifying and acceptable to you." You see, my dearest wife, how handsomely this has been done. I see in the Madras paper it runs—Harness Gent. to be Ensign, and should it be gazetted in the same manner it will be no difficult matter to pass it off for one of his cousins. My only anxiety arises from the fear it might make him less diligent in his studies. I hope this step will be pleasing to my dearest Bessy although it makes a very old woman of her to have a son in the army. I long to hear that Charles is at some eligible school, but I hope to hear it at home.

10 February 1801

I think you will see with me the propriety of keeping secret from dear Charles his appointment to the Ensigncy. I mean to write immediately to endeavor to purchase him a Lieutenancy and then to put him on the half pay. It will go far towards his education, and will in no way hinder him from entering upon any other profession; and should he prefer that of a soldier he will not have the drudgery of the lower ranks.

The teaching of the two little girls weighed more lightly on their parent's mind, though he took a keen and loving interest in their various accomplishments:

Our little Jane is I trust improving in her reading. You say she carrys herself prettily and that her manners are perfect, which must delight me. The lightest shade of vulgarity in our daughters would assassinate me. I could almost as unfeelingly see her affected, but my Bessy will teach them her own ease, nature and truth. I think they should never go to school. We will get masters for every thing you cannot teach. We cannot give them up for an affected school and I promise myself so great happiness in and with my family.

The drawings of our dear girls gave me very great pleasure. You know how much I have been always pleased with this lovely art. I long to see our Jane and Little Bessy cultivate it. It leads so readily to observe the beauties of nature in her most beautiful works; You must see how every tree branches, the shape of its leaves, their colour, under every light and season. They will the better taste also the delightful descriptions of the best Poets, and at once see where they deviate from nature.

With reading, writing, drawing, and the poets—to say nothing of hemming and making stockings—Jane and Jemima were evidently to become two very cultivated little girls. Geography too was not forgotten.

I expect to see a very dear little daughter very clever and very good. She will read to me very often. I think it will be a very good amusement to find all the places we read about in the news papers and in the Gazette, to learn what sort of places they severally are, and we will get some globes and find them on it in an instant from the longitudes and latitudes given us. We shall then know whether they are hot or cold, whether it is winter or summer there, or day or night. I think little Jemima will like to know all that her sister does and will be one of our party.

William Harness's second stay in Trincomali (which had now become " this detested country ") was to be a short one. On 10 February 1800 the regiment was preparing for an " unknown destination ".

Colonel Wellesley is here; he is going on an expedition, but where is the enemy? We have none in India. He was not allowed to storm Seringapatam, although the Governor General's brother, because there was risk, but he has followed Doondiah and his unarmed tribe all over Mysore and my Lord Wellesley has sounded his praises. He is a very aimable man, and I have a great esteem for him, but the army don't forgive his taking the Command of Seringapatam without sharing the dangers of the Capture. He laughs at his expedition, he takes but four Regiments with him, and has been so flattering as to select ours as one. It is said to be against Ternate and one or two of the Eastern Islands that have fitted out privateers to annoy our trade. You will see the success blazed off by the Governor General. A Sea Trip will be a pleasant thing and we are to return to the Coast and leave this vile place. I think we cannot be longer away than two months. For the sake of our young men I am heartily glad. They have been too long cut off from all society and rationality. I fancyed I discovered a frightful falling off on my return to them.

The eventual destination proved to be, not the small island of Ternate nor the capture of Java and Mauritius as originally planned, but Egypt. The four battalions prepared by Wellesley in Ceylon for the capture of the islands were switched over, when long delayed orders arrived at Calcutta, to another scene of Napoleon's machinations. On 3 April the Colonel sent a note from Bombay telling of some presents that he had " committed to the charge " of a friend to take home: a gold Box containing

three Trichinopoly chains and two rings. The Box I bought in the Nizam's Army a few days after the capture of Seringapatam. Captain Evans is sending the silver bird.[1] It is very clumsy but bought by myself in Tippoo's palace, you will perhaps for its intrinsic value excuse its want of beauty.

I have been here two days and embark to-morrow for Mocha with General Baird, five Regiments being destined for Upper Egypt to cut off the Supplies which the French have drawn from it, while Sir R. Abercrombie fights them. I hope to get home without revisiting this country.

So on to Egypt which was, at any rate—or so it seemed at the time—a good step nearer home.

---

[1] The " clumsy " silver bird, two chains, and two rings are still in the possession of my family. *C.M.D.-J.*

9

Egypt

1800—1801—1802—1803: the slow years passed by—years of
alternating hope and disappointment. Again and again an
early return home seemed almost certain. Again and again
some obstacle intervened. And as often as postponement of that
joyful day was threatened, after the first burst of frustration
and despair, William Harness, faithful and hopeful as ever,
found consolation and resignation and renewed confidence.

The Egyptian expedition, destined to capture the French
army left in that country, was under the command of Colonel
Harness's good friend, General—afterwards Sir David—Baird.
Arthur Wellesley, who had been appointed second-in-com-
mand, was taken ill at Bombay and had to be left behind—
providentially as it proved, for the ship in which he was to
have sailed went down with all hands. It was due therefore to
General Baird's resource and intrepidity that the army from
India achieved its wearing and difficult march, across a hundred
miles of desert and through wholly unknown country, from
Qusair on the Red Sea to the eastern bank of the Nile. Colonel
Murray was sent ahead in order to send back supplies of water
and provisions to different stations on the route; and parties
of sepoys were employed in searching for springs and digging
wells. William Harness, always reticent where personal hardships were concerned, gave few hints at the problems surmounted on that adventurous trek.

Kenne [1] on the Nile, 7 July 1801

A line from me from *Egypt* will surprize you. However I
am in the most perfect health, after crossing the Desert from
Cossir. [2] The different modes of spelling these places will
perhaps puzzle you, but the latter you will find a port in the

[1] Qena.   [2] Qusair.

156

Red Sea in 28 Degrees of Latitude, and this in nearly the same parallel and about a hundred and fifty miles to the Westward. I have but 200 of the 80th with me, but command the 88th which form my right wing. Mr Harvey is with me and has just swam across the Nile, a proof of health. Everything is in over flowing abundance. We were obliged to carry our water across the Desert but my Battalion were the great part of the road mounted on Camels, the first British Corps probably that ever made the route. The heat almost intolerable but not at all injuring the health of my people. At Juddah [1] I accompany'd General Baird in his visit to the Xeriff of Mecca, and was presented by him with a Shawl which I should be delighted to wrap round you the first cold day.

General Baird's army travelled down the Nile in boats to join General Hutchinson (who had succeeded Sir Ralph Abercromby), but arrived too late by just three days to take part in the surrender of Cairo—a disappointing end to that epic journey. The French commander, General Belliard, agreed to evacuate Cairo and to remove his army of nearly 14,000 back to France. At a camp near Rozetta William Harness received the news that he was once more—and this time with no mistake—Lieutenant-Colonel of a regiment.

4 September 1801

Here I am travelling over the land of Egypt with every circumstance of fatigue that ever poor pilgrim experienced. We came down the Nile to Geeza [2] in Country boats; small as they are I had an hundred and fifty soldiers in mine, we arrived there just in time to hear of the surrender of Grand Cairo, and encamped on the Island of Rhoda,[3] that separates those two places. We came on to this place and Alexandria fell the day following, so that our services can have availed nothing more than what a knowledge of such a reinforcement within reach might have had on the enemy. General Baird is just returned from a visit to Sir John Hutchinson and tells me I am Lt. Colonel of the 80th; if so my Bessy will have seen it long ago.

[1] Jedda in Arabia.
[2] Giza.
[3] Elroda or Gezirat (Island), an island in the Nile between Cairo and Giza.

The Nile is a broad muddy river with small creaks at intervals running from each side. It is now at its greatest height and by means of wheels turned by oxen the water is raised from it, and the creaks branching from it, in sufficient quantities to water the country in many places as far as four miles from it, all along its course. The remainder of Egypt from the Cataracks (for part of my Battalion was sent to them to impress boats) to the Mediterranean (which is now in sight) is wild, barren rocks and vast deserts without vegitation or water. Such is Egypt. This narrow slip of cultivated ground is extremely abundant in corn, fruits and the garden productions that they attempt to raise on it. The Towns that read so pompous are miserable. Grand Cairo to view it from the Citadel strikes you with wonder from its extent and the almost innumerable habitations it contains; but there is not a street in it, that would admit of a post chaise being driven through it, was so unknown a thing as a wheeled carriage to make its appearance in any part of Egypt that I have seen. I past a day in visiting the famed piramids of Geeza. The only idea they invited was that so much labor should have been thrown away in productions of neither use, beauty or profit. I rode for several hours through the principal streets of Cairo wishing to purchase something worth taking home for my Bessy, our children, our house or even myself, but could not find a thing that was worth the carriage. The impositions that are practised exceed all the villany of Europe. I have an Arab Servant who lived three years with a French General, who interprets for me and guards me much. The Soldiers have been very much afflicted with sore eyes, probably from the night airs to which their duty has necessarily exposed them.

We have seen few of the Army from England. They appear very dirty, starved and shabby, not having any wine or comforts, even cloaths, with them. They were surprized at our manner of living. We brought even cooks for the Soldiers from India, and, much as we were put to it for carriage, took care to bring a few dozens of Madiera across the Desert. Colonel Champagné has not been heard of since the 1st March from Goa, when he wrote that he was detained repairing his water Casks. He had before he left Trincomallee applyed for sick leave to go home. These are supposed by those that don't know him not to be the acts of a brave man going on service. I am heartily glad that he has left us. The system of peculation and ruin that had crept in, I hope unseen by him, because always unchecked, had become a subject for conversation in every part of India. We shall soon know what is to be our destination. I fear it will be to garrison Egypt for some months for the wind will not be favorable for the army to return by the Red Sea till March.

Like a chorus to every letter there occurred the problem of the still unpaid prize money. Even the loss of the expected home leave in the early months of 1801, " which Colonel Champagné most indecently refused me ", had had its brighter side, since it gave opportunities for further inquiries after this payment " so unaccountably delayed ". Often he weighed the question—should he go home without it? That would have been to abandon the hope of a gracious, modest ease for his beloved family, and of the blissful home life, free from financial worries, to which he ever looked forward; for the difficulties of sending money to England were immense and agents were not to be trusted. Or should he wait just a little longer—only a few months at the most—and return with the prize safely in his possession? It was the latter course that he chose; and, unfortunate as the decision proved to be, who can say that he was mistaken?

Camp near Rozetta, 4 September 1801

Untill I hear that it is [paid] I should not be acting as I feel worthy your husband, but regardless of the interests of our children, to attempt to ask leave, Month has passed after month untill years have elapsed in a way that no foresight could calculate. The almost wearing anxiety I have to get [home], the length of absence and the cheated hopes, so warm and so illusory, these ideas all flow mixed with melancholy that depresses my spirits almost to tears. It has been a painful delay but it has given me my promotion, a Commission for our dear Boy and two thousand pagodas.

Painful indeed, but he was quick, as always, to note the compensations.

Napoleon himself had left Egypt in 1799, and in January of

the following year the French invaders had come to an agreement with the Turks by which they undertook to quit the country. Here the British Government had intervened and insisted that, if the convention were carried out, the French must be treated as prisoners. The agreement therefore fell through and the French remained. Now in 1801 they were commanded by Baron de Menou, who had professed himself a follower of the Prophet. This had gained him some popularity, which was quickly lost when he declared Egypt to be a French protectorate. The conquest of Alexandria, which Colonel Harness so narrowly missed, brought about the end of the French occupation, since Menou was forced to agree to the removal of his forces. We hear nothing of this in William Harness's letters. It may well be that some of them were lost—as happened not infrequently—but he often appears carefully to have avoided over much reference to public events. For instance on 6 November he wrote:

You will ere you receive this have read the tragical end of the unfortunate Beys.[1] The rigidity with which I, at all times when on service, conceive it duty to observe silence on all operations of a public nature, confines me here to mute pity.

Camp near Rozetta, 30 September 1801

Settled in Camp here we have little communication with the *English* Army but by a few of our Friends visiting us. I don't know why but we are not popular at Alexandria. The very considerable difference that exists in point of allowances may have caused a jealousy, but why among reasonable men and gentlemen and who have no determination or even vote is unaccountable. It is decreed that the Indian Army is to make a part of the Garrison of Egypt. Lord Cavan is left in command, he past a few days here with Lord William Bentinck who told me had left London six weeks from that day. Good God! my Bessy, how short a period. Sir John Hutchinson writes that it is not the intention to send this army again to India, but that the King's Regiments are to go home; may the event

[1] This treacherous betrayal of the principal Beys (governors of provinces) was carried out by the Turkish High Admiral acting on orders from Constantinople. He invited them to an entertainment on his flagship and they were either murdered on board or fired at in open boats.

prove so. I find in the Gazette my promotion took place on the 2nd May; how very happy has the beginning of that month more than once made me. Colonel Montressor commands our Brigade. He is nearly a year a senior Lt. Col. to me and was in the same predicament with myself, having been appointed to a Lt. Colonelcy in India and not confirmed at home. He is very gentlemanly and his reputation stands high as an Officer.

We are out at exercise from day light to nine o'Clock, nearly four hours, every morning. The Troops live remarkably well. Every man has a quart of excellent coffee for breakfast with plenty of bread and cold meat. His Soup at dinner cannot be better with an abundant quantity of good beef or mutton and a pint of wine. He has also three pence a day to spend.

I hope Charles is at School. I have not yet seen his name in the army list. If I can get home from here I will bring my little horse with me. He is a great favorite, and I should like to give him over to my dear Boy. Does [Jane] learn to dance. As I am now so near she will oblige me by writing me a letter to tell me all she does and learns. I expect to see a good little clever girl, very prettily behaved, because very natural in all she does, and that she will be able to tell me almost as much as I can of all the places I have seen. I wish I had here a pair of her comfortable stockings for I am told the winter will be wet and cold. We are furnishing our men with European Cloathing but the heat of the middle of the day is very great. We are on a sand which denys even vegetation to moss or a weed.

Colonel Harness went on to describe how many British soldiers had died of the Plague during the last fall of the Nile; but he appeared little troubled by any fear of " this afflictive malady ", which, although " Allarming at a distance, when near seems to make not even a subject for precaution ". General Baird had " established every wholesome regulation " and Colonel Harness had " seen several of the french who declare they have had it five or six times, and that it is so well known to the medical men that in the hands of some it proves fatal to not more than one in ten ". Obviously there was nothing here to worry an anxious wife in far away Derbyshire! What troubled him more was the fact that he heard nothing of the sailings of ships to England, so that often one sailed without carrying a letter from him. " General Hutchinson is not particularly civil in this respect."

It is likely that Mrs Harness found it hard to make up her mind to the parting with her first-born, and it was not until early in 1801 that Charles was placed, as his father wished, in a school " where his Education, health and morals, as well as manners will be best secured". It was still another year before William Harness received the news of this important and anxiously awaited step in his small son's life. Elizabeth had chosen carefully and Mr Heyrick's school at Leicester had a very good name; but the boy's first letter home was calculated to wring a mother's heart. In an uneven, blotted, childish hand (though the letter is singularly free from the " blunders " he mentions) Charles wrote:

My very very dear Mama,

I write you these lines to tell you that yesterday morning I felt a violent pain in my head, which continued from that time till I came into School in the evening. Master Hill said that it was the custom for every boy when he had anything the matter with him to tell Mr Heyrick. I did so, he felt my pulse, and asked me whether my head felt hot. I said it did and thereupon he told me to keep as still as possible that night and to-day I feel very sick and ill. When I saw you on Thursday I did not think it was the last time of seeing you, therefore I did not kiss you, but I hope I shall see you and my sisters again before you leave Oadby as I think it my duty to kiss you, dear Mama. You have not sent me my French Grammar, as I want it to get my lesson.

Have you heard from dear Papa and send my love to Aunty when you see her. Send a thousand kisses to Jane and Jemima. Excuse the many blunders I have made as my tears confused me very much.

Adieu my dear Mama,

Believe me I am and always shall be

Your truly affectionate and dutiful son

C. P. W. Harness

P.S. Pray answer my letter to come by Mr Mile. I am very glad to hear you are all well.

Before long he was writing in a happier vein.

Leicester, 11 April 1801

I am glad to tell you that I am in good health, and like school very well, also I go on with my French very well; I am glad to hear that James Walch dined with you, and I did not wonder at Jane and Jemima being glad because we always were so when he came. There is going to be a speaking day soon, and the four headboys will speak, and the Mayor and Corporation will come and hear them.

A letter written to " Aunty Croke " gives a cheerful picture of nursery life at Dronfield.

Dear Aunty,

I thank you very much for your kind letter and the half-crown. I am very well. Pray write to me soon and tell Jane to write soon. I should like very much to be in the band to call you to breakfast now; I suppose little Jemima plays on the little trumpet.

Another letter to his aunt shows the obstacles in the way of returning home for the holidays.

I do not know how I am to get home without I go by Derby, and then I must go by myself, without any body comes for me. All the Chaises etc. will be taken for people to go to Nottingham to vote, and if I do get a place in the Coach, I shall not be able to get through Nottingham for the mob, so that I must go by Derby for I cannot go any other way.

The small boy was shaping well and becoming keen, considerate, and self-reliant.

By the beginning of November there were rumours in Egypt of peace. (The short-lived and uneasy Peace of Amiens, which gave Napoleon a convenient breathing space, was signed on 27 March 1802.)

Camp near El Hamed,[1] 6 November 1801

We have a very strong report of a peace coming through three or four unconnected channels. I find it so generally

[1] El Hammad.

credited at Alexandria, that an Aide du Camp of Sir John Hutchinson's and Colonel Cole are going home by the way of France. I never was so long without hearing from you; the last letter is dated 20th August 1800. We have heard nothing from India since we left Bombay early in April. Colonel Champagné and the half of the Regiment with him never appeared. I have heard nothing from my agent, but the monsoon is changing and we shall soon receive our letters.

Nothing, he said, would induce him to go home by way of India if leave could be granted from Egypt (subject always to provision that the prize money had been paid). He believed that this leave could be granted by General Baird.

I can say it to you without being accused of vanity, there is no Officer in this army, out of his own family, so often at his table or that enjoys more his confidence. He has done me the honour to select me to manage two or three things where it was necessary to repose a full confidence and he has been satisfied with the issue. He wrote to me from Alexandria to tell me he had seen my promotion in the monthly army list, and on his barely seeing it in the paper, he put me in orders allowing me to draw all the emoluments of the Regiment from the 2nd May.

Could I but see my account settled I shall have nothing to keep me from you. How shall I enjoy my dear home after eight years of serious toils, and with what satisfaction shall I look back that no part of it has been left undone. My Services have not been brilliant but they have been very arduous.

His good friend, General Baird, was to give further proof of his trust when the time came to leave Egypt.

In January 1802 the regiment was at Alexandria. Colonel Harness lived at first in an apartment in the house of Lord Cavan. "It is the one formerly occupied by Buonaparte." Later he moved to that in which the French General Menou had lived. There was much coming and going and the thought of home leave was in the air. On 13 January he sent a short note to tell Elizabeth that he had been appointed a temporary Brigadier.

Cleopatra's Needle was arousing a good deal of interest.

Alexandria, 20 January

Every effort is making to carry home one of the Needles of
Cleopatra. A warf is forming for the purpose of embarking it
and a Ship is to be cut down to receive it. The needle is one
solid piece of granite, the weight of it is estimated at two
hundred tuns independent of the base. You know it is full of
Hieroglyphics on every side. Three thousand pounds was
subscribed here in two days to pay the expence of carrying
this very curious present to his Majesty in commemoration of
the splendid victories obtained in this part of the world by his
fleets and army.

I have before told you how little I have observed to repay
the curiosity of a traveller who visits Egypt. At that time I
had not seen Alexandria. Pompey's pillar is a most magnificent
object. This town shews evident marks of pristine grandeur,
but it is now little more than a rude heap of ruins. The
materials of its aqueducts, temples, libraries and splendid
edifices have been wrought by barbarous hands into shapeless
habitations of ignorant Turks and rapacious Jews, but are now
crumbling into dust and serve to bury many feet in the earth
the more solid remains of its former greatness.

Life in Alexandria was not idle, for there were courts martial,
which William Harness found " odious ", committees of inquiry
and many other matters to occupy an officer's time; yet there
was evidently a certain lightening of strain, a feeling almost as
of a school breaking up for the holidays. Colonel Harness
was able to give a " very comfortable " dinner to his General
and some other officers. " He says the best he has eaten in
Egypt; it was not expensive." Theatricals are mentioned of
which William Harness was appointed manager; and on 2
April he gave an enthusiastic report of a highly festive occasion.

I told you we were preparing to give a dinner to the Garrison
on the 21st of March. A hundred and sixty sat down, it would
be to write a little volume to give you an account of it. It
was really splendid. The room was lighted by five hundred
lamps besides chandeliers. Ever greens decked with artificial
flowers formed avenues for the tables. The Coup d'oeil on
the entrance was sensibly felt. I will send you two of the

Transparencies drawn by Montresor. The names of all the General Officers who commanded Brigades were entwined in a wreathe of laurel encircled with a blaze of glory. Lord Cavan made us a very handsome speech of thanks. It was one of the prettiest things I ever saw. Lord Cavan dined with me a few days after and expressed himself as having dined on fairy land. Our theatricals have succeeded beyond expectation.

Letters from England began to arrive more speedily. Elizabeth too had her servant troubles to report, for her husband writes: " I am greatly surprized and am concerned to find out Molly has turned out so idle. There was the appearance of honesty about her that I took for honesty itself."

In February the father's anxiety about his son's education was set at rest by hearing that the boy was under the care of the excellent master at Leicester.

Alexandria, 25 February 1802

Conceive with what happiness I received your Letter of the 30th November after so dismal an age. A few days before had put me in possession of yours of the 24th April, with the account of our dear Charles being with Mr Heyrick. I was reading over the account of Charles's engagement to Col. Ruddisdele [1] (who is from that part of Nottinghamshire that borders upon Leicester), when he stopt me by saying " are you so fortunate, Harness, as to have your son with Heyrick? He is the very man if I had a son I should choose to educate him. He was the tutor of Lord Apthorpe and selected by my friend Lord Spenser as the fittest man to bring up his son. They have given him a good living, but I fancy have not done with him yet." Fancy me, my Bessy, greedily devouring every syllable of this charming account. I find dear Charles's commission is in the Gazette, and — Harness Gentleman without a Christian name, so that you can use your pleasure about concealing or revealing it. The purchase of the Lieutenancy will be nearly paid for from the amount of his pay. The half pay will go a good way for several years towards paying for his education.

[1] Described in another letter as " a most elegant minded man ".

So the future of the little officer appeared assured.

At the end of April reliable news came from Italy of the confirmation of peace. By that time Colonel Harness had definitely decided that he must return to England via India. The faithful Zamor was to be sent home to await his master at Dronfield, since his health was unlikely to stand a further stay in that country. " Zamor will, I hope, be very useful in hearing our little Girls their French lessons."

Alexandria, 27 April 1802

I am ordered to Gezah to relieve Colonel Ramsey and leave Alexandria the day after to-morrow. The extremely gratifying and confidential manner in which General Baird has left to me the whole arrangement of the march of the Army Guns and stores with the provision department untill their embarkation at Suez is flattering to me in the highest degree. My first object will be to establish depots at the halting places on the desert, and to see them well supplied with provisions and water. You see I am not to be idle. I shall fix my Head Quarters at Gezah. The instant I get to India my Soul will dictate to me to hasten with every possible despatch to the arms of my adored wife.

This " very arduous " and responsible undertaking was successfully carried out. On the 20 May, when the army had reached " Birket el Hudge ",[1] Colonel Harness was able to report that " The General is much pleased at the several arrangements and the rapidity with which they have been carried into effect ". Young Mr Harvey, for whom in spite of his many failures and extravagances William Harness always felt a certain interest and responsibility, was still far from learning wisdom.

I was in hopes Mr Harvey would have contrived to have so well pleased Colonel Ramsey as to have his interest for a company in his Regiment, but I find they do not part good friends. He told the Colonel at his table the other day that " he had a right to give him advice ". I fear he was exercising his right a

---

[1] Colonel Harness's spelling. Possibly Birket-el-Hagg (Pool of the Pilgrim), ten miles north-east of Cairo.

little injudiciously. Colonel Ramsey has served near half a century, and his experience is no bad support to a natural good understanding.

By 5 June the desert crossing was safely accomplished and William Harness was ready to embark at Suez.

The general is going on board at 12 o'Clock and I follow the day after to-morrow. We had yesterday the most superb fête I ever saw on board of ship, given by Sir Home Popham in the Romney; all served off massive plate, the cabin fitted up with the richest satin. The Effendi was of our party.

I go in the Calcutta a most beautiful Ship; my Cabin is very comfortable and the Captain has the reputation of a good accomodating and obliging man. I take three horses with me. We shall have a fair wind all the way, for the wind here is not that inconstant thing it is with you.

But alas, for the good ship *Calcutta* and her accommodating and obliging captain! for the next news is of shipwreck. From El Tor in Arabia on 17 June Colonel Harness wrote:

Through the inattention of our Captain he suffered our ship to go on Shore. She will in all probability be lost, but Sir Home Popham took every body out of her, and brought us over here at the foot of Mount Sinai and Horeb, where we await a King's Ship, the Wilhelmina, from Suez to take us on. We are all well, feasting on the fine fruits that grow on this much celebrated holy mount. We expect to embark in about a week and shall then proceed to Madras. It is impossible to exceed the civilities of Sir Home Popham. There is a Priest of the Greek Church, a fine venerable figure, who bows us down with kind hospitalities. I had calculated to go home in the Calcutta, she was so fine a Ship, but her unheedy Captain run her into a fine soft bed of sand. The dear Romney's boats soon took us on board and Sir Home brought us to this watering place about sixty miles from Suez.

We know from subsequent letters that Colonel Harness lost all his baggage in the wreck, and he learnt in October that the

Government would allow no compensation.[1] What became of the three horses is not told. In the short note to Elizabeth, designed doubtless to spare her feelings, the loss of the ship appears as a mild and, on the whole, not unpleasant adventure, and the sojourn by Mount Sinai as a lively picnic. It appeared far otherwise in the official report which the Colonel wrote for General Baird. He was considerably annoyed when he discovered that this " dismal account " had found its way into the English newspapers.

Tor, 15 June, 1802

Sir,

I have much concern in acquainting you that the Calcutta Transport with three hundred and thirty one of His Majesty's 80th regiment . . . and seventy nine native Indian followers, was wrecked at three o'Clock A.M. on the 13th instant on the Egyptian shore in lat. 28 deg. 33 min.

The distance from the Shore when she first struck did not appear more than half a mile; it was blowing fresh, the Sea ran high, and the surf beat with so much violence against her Stern, that the planks of her cabin were almost instantaneously stowed in, her upper Masts were cut away and in attempting to get out the boats, one of them was swampt. As her situation was deemed critical I ordered an Officer and 30 men into the long boat, hoping that they would make the Shore, but with the most lively pain I saw her swampt from the wreck: a Sergeant and six privates were drowned, and the rest fortunately swam ashore.

We had now no boat remaining; the gale increased; she was reported to have made six feet water, and her Officers were not without apprehensions of her going to pieces. At seven o'Clock three Ships appeared in sight, but so much to the leeward, that with the Sea and wind with which they had to contend, little hope was entertained of their affording any assistance. However we soon discovered one of the vessels to be His Majesty's Ship Romney, which about ten o'Clock anchored at about two miles and a half from the Calcutta,

---

[1] No compensation was allowed during Colonel Harness's lifetime, but it appears from one of his son's letters that about the year 1811 " £100 was granted by his Majesty for my dear Father's loss of Baggage in the Red Sea ".

when Sir Home Popham directed the Dutchess of York to anchor at a middle distance from us; and at twelve the Romney's Launch came on board: by nine in the Evening every man of the 80th except the seven drowned in the long boat, was taken on board the Romney.

It is to the skilful position Sir Home Popham took up, so as to enable his boats to fall to and from the wreck: to the excellence of his boats . . . and it is to the dexterity and perseverance of his well trained boats' crew, we are eminently indebted for the preservation of so many lives.

The humane personal attention of Sir Home Popham to the comfort of the Troops, many of whom reached the Romney in a very weakly state, will long be remembered with the warmest gratitude.

The difficult rescue was not effected without considerable danger to the brave rescuers.

On the morning of the 14th, the Romney having dragged her Anchorage, Sir Home cut his Cable and ran for this Bay leaving the Dutchess of York to take on board any baggage that might be accidentally saved from the wreck. The sea had reached her main deck before the last division of the Detachment left her.

At this place they found " shelter from the Sun and weather in a few buildings inhabited by fishermen "; and in these the 80th awaited the arrival of the *Wilhelmina*.

10

Return to India

COLONEL HARNESS had confidently expected that, his business at Madras happily settled, he would take the first available ship for England—possibly even the *Wilhelmina* which had brought him in " a pleasant voyage " from El Tor after his shipwreck. Little did he foresee how he would be " the sport of cross accidents ", which would involve him in another sixteen months in India and some of the hardest fighting that he had as yet experienced. At Calcutta, where in September 1802 he spent several days, he found a gay social life and he himself received a " very flattering " reception.

8 September

I arrived at seven in the evening and Lord Wellesley sent to desire I would dine with him as I was, that it was a private day. He at dinner requested I would live with him, but as I excused myself on the occupation I should have for the short stay I had to make at the seat of the Supreme Government, he told me a plate would be reserved for me every day, and in the morning an Aide du Camp called on me by His Excellency's command to hope I would dine at the Government house whenever I was disengaged. In the after dinner we went to Mrs Barlow's where General Baird introduced me to every body, and the next day I had visits from all the Presidency and invitations to the 1st October. It is a scene of constant dissipation. However I contrive to get on horse back every morning at 5 o'Clock; the General sends me a horse.

Many people believe I am doing a very mad thing to go home, with the prospects they say I have before me, but they know not my Bessy, nor the happiness a mediocrity, a almost paucity of fortune has to bestow spent with her.

171

The prospects of an immediate return had already receded, but he expected to be able to embark at the end of December " which will ensure a good climate all the way home ". For all Lord Wellesley's " Strong assurances ", the payment of the prize money still hung fire. By this time, however, he had acquired nearly £6000 (an " acknowledged error " on the part of his agents at Madras had restored to him 2000 pagodas), " so that the Prize money will not be an object of very alarming regret ". In spite of the extraordinary dilatoriness on the part of the Government in the matter of compensation for his lost " cloaths " he evidently fitted himself out with a fairly extensive wardrobe, for in the following May he had to tell a truly tragic story of a further loss.

My dear Jane making a shirt! I believe I shall be almost necessitated to get her to make shirts for me. Eighteen complete suits of cloaths with all my table cloaths but two (bought in Bengal to bring home), sheets, dressing gowns &c &c &c with my poor washerman's wife and four children were washed down a nullah.[1] They were sleeping in the dry bed of it, when the torrent came down with such impetuosity as to sweep all before it. Many lost their lives. In the vicinity of the mountains a shower is sufficient to produce these melancholy effects.

At the end of December, far from setting off for home, William Harness had to break the news to his wife of another delay—caused by a new and honourable call to duty and a further responsibility, which may to some extent have sweetened the disappointment.

Madras, 26 December 1802

I have taken my passage in the Ann & Amelia to sail very early in the next month, the finest season of the year. Still, my adored wife, my Voyage will I fear be for a short period delayed. In a manner that I cannot reflect on but with pride General Stuart has offered me the Command of a Brigade in an armament of observation that is forming. I am living, and have lived for the last two months with General Baird on terms of the purest confidence. I receive from him every mark

[1] Dry water-course.

172

of friendship. The General is to command one wing. The purpose is to overawe the rebellious Marattas and to place the Paishwar on the Musnad.[1] He has consented to all our terms and to receive in Poona an auxiliary force. I trust the delay will be but for a very short period. General Baird is advertizing all his furniture, carriages &c to be sold, meaning to return to Europe the moment he quits the field. He leaves the nomination of my Brigade Major to myself. I had sold my horses but after so flattering an offer (none of the 80th take the field) should you, *my Bessy*, have thought me so worthy of you could I have refused. I have not to tell you what I feel at this disappointment short as *I believe* my stay in India will be. Shall I join you more worthy of you? I felt with so large a force in the field, although there is the strongest possible reasons to believe all will be adjusted with Holkar by negotiation, that my character might suffer by my taking such a moment to leave India.

It is still not impossible that the Maratta business may be terminated without a march of the army; but I conceive it unlikely as the appearance of so large a force would be very availing to produce harmony among a disjoined confederacy.

The " Maratta business " was very far from being " terminated without a march of the Army ", and on 21 February 1803 William Harness was at Chitteldroog. With General Baird he had been " marching most rapidly " for nearly six weeks to join General Wellesley and General Campbell. His financial situation was, he considered, improving—an improvement that denoted very careful management in view of the astonishing number of servants that were necessary.

I leave all the pay I draw from the 80th Regiment to be paid into the hands of my Agent, about a hundred and seventy pagodas a month, and live on my staff allowance, which it requires great management to do. Of every description I have fifty one servants, thirty seven oxen and three horses and find my establishment actually inadequate to what they have to perform. My Brigade Major and Assistant Quarter Master

[1] " *Musnud.* A seat made of cushions; especially one used as a throne by the native Princes of India." (*Oxford English Dictionary*.)

General are considered of my family or personal staff. I am obliged to put on my table Claret, Madeira, port, Beer and custom has lately added liqueurs; and all this with hams, cheese &c &c and all china articles to be brought nearly five hundred miles from Madras. If I were to mention in this Camp that I save money it would be to risk my credit for I am said to live well; but I am very regular in looking after my servants and settle with my Butler daily. Col. St John and I always dine together alternately when disengaged. General Baird told me yesterday he would dine with me to-day—we sometimes join dinners. I will tell you what my Servants are and Zamor will explain them to you. I have 14 Palankeen Bearers, four of them carry my breakfast Trunk; a Maistry [1] and 10 Bullock men including two Bandy [2] Currers,[3] a Tindal [4] and eight Tent Lascars.[5] I furnish my own tents for which I receive 30 pagodas a month; 6 Coolies, 6 Horse Keepers and Grass cutters; A Butler, Cloaths Boy, two Mettys [6] and a Cook. I don't include my Puncaully [7] as he is paid by the public, nor six men I am allowed to carry my flag. I have not a single man for state or one I can do without. My Lascars do also the work of Coolies. Conceive the concourse of followers that must attend an India army.

In March 1803, much to his sorrow, Colonel Harness had to bid farewell to " that great character ", and beloved friend, General Baird. He had greatly enjoyed the General's companionship. " His kindnesses are very great. I either breakfast or dine with him every day and we ride together every evening. He is very warm hearted, strictly honorable and firm in his attachments." In January they had together paid an interesting visit to the sons of Tippoo Sultan.

[1] Foreman or bullock owner.

[2] Bullock carriage, buggy, or cart.

[3] Currer—probably anglicized from the Telugu *kurra*—a boy.

[4] Native petty officer of Lascars.

[5] Lascar in Anglo-Indian—a tent-pitcher.

[6] *Metty*—an assistant under the head servant (usually a house servant, washes up, attends to lamps, etc.).

[7] *Puncaully*—water carrier.

Camp near Vellore, 21 January

I am just returned from a visit I have been making with General Baird to Tippoo's four eldest sons. They live in a kind of state, but their palace is a prison, and every attendant a spy, even their letters undergo the inspection of the Commandant before they are suffered to be despatched. Futty Hyder the Eldest has very courtly manners, and he is said to be very well informed. Their houses and families are separate, they are allowed too a liberal establishment so that their misery is splendid. Colonel Dallas commands and accompanied us. He has all the harshness of a Gaoler. Col. Doveton who was supposed to use towards them too much mildness, and who had been by Lord Cornwallis selected to take charge of the two junior as hostages was removed from Vellore to make way for the present Commandant two years ago.

The happy comradeship of these two officers was now over. As far back as 1799 there had been friction between the General and Colonel Wellesley, as he then was. General Baird had been Tippoo Sultan's prisoner in Seringapatam for four years. He successfully led the storming of that ruler's capital, Colonel Wellesley being in charge of the reserve. When the Governor-General appointed his brother to the honourable and lucrative post of Governor of Seringapatam, and Baird, the senior officer, was passed over, he not unnaturally felt considerably aggrieved. Now trouble arose again. " I have experienced ", wrote William Harness on 23 March 1803, " the most profound regret in the loss of my very excellent friend, General Baird. He left, I hear, General Stuart's army in disgust on General Wellesley being ordered on with the advance of his own choosing."

Conceive how greatly I was flattered in seeing myself second to General Wellesley with the strongest European Regiment and upwards of four thousand men in my Brigade, and that Brigade in the advance. I believe so many effective men were not left for the nominal wing left to General Baird to command. He goes to Europe immediately, and will probably write to you on his arrival. I rode back the day of the two camps separating to take a farewell dinner. Nothing could be more

175

friendly. We shall be on the Kistna the 31st and expect to be in the neighbourhood of Poona by the middle of April. Fortunately every Maratta we have seen is a friend, they come in every day offering to serve with from 500 to a 1000 Horse. They conceive we are invincible, and are ready to give in to whatever General Wellesley dictates. The respect paid to persons and property is as great as if we had an English jury to decide on all our acts.

He went on to tell how he had saved General Baird from a somewhat awkward situation:

The General, very far from his custom, had given what I knew not to be the order he intended, and the Troops were getting into embarrassment. I instantly rode where the confusion began and rectifyed it, brought them into line and sent orders for the whole wing. Genl Baird saw what he intended should be done was done, contrary to his own orders, that he had discovered the error in, and was apprehensive it would be seen by Wellesley.

General Baird wrote to William Harness from Bangalore on 23 March:

I had the highest gratification on receiving your most kind and friendly letter of the 15th. I will not now touch on that most unpleasant subject of my being forced to leave the Army. I trust the world at large and his R. Highness in particular, will do me the justice to allow it was impossible I could stay with *honor* to myself or with *advantage* to my Country. . . . By all accounts war with France is inevitable. Orders arrived just in the nick of time to keep possession of the Cape of Good Hope, for it was to have been delivered up that Evening. All the Troops had embarked excepting the Guards. . . . Genl Stuart I found had nothing to do with arrangements. I parted with him on the best terms. He regretted much my leaving the Army and gave me leave to go in a very handsome manner.

This serious disagreement between the two generals, both so able and courageous, both so high-minded, must have been a

176

sore trial to William Harness. Wellesley was the respected and admired leader, Baird the revered and intimate friend. It was with General Wellesley that during the next months his lot was to be cast.

In the first and, as it proved to be, the last letter that little Jane received from her father he put very simply the dilemma that still kept him away from his children. It is a charming letter; as usual her parent is much concerned with the little girl's progress in geography.

Camp between the Gulperba and Kistna,
28 March 1803

My very dear Jane,

One of my great uneasinesses is to be so often disappointed after trying the assistance of all my friends to get leave to come home; and when I had attained permission, that these naughty Marattas should follow the steps of the wicked French, and drive their prince from his palace and capital, was so unexpected a thing and so shameful, that I was afraid I should be thought not to have done my duty, to go home till this poor prince is put again on his throne. In all the Countries we pass through his Chiefs come to visit us and present us with Shawls. I wish they would give me something prettier for my Jane. We expect soon to be at Poona, his capital, perhaps as I shall have been there, you will look in the Map, and see what other great Towns he has, and what rivers we have to pass. Read in the Gazeteer the account of all his principal places and what they produce. If the rivers have any communication with the Sea, we shall be able to get wine and Tea and sugar from Bombay, for it would be very uncomfortable to get all these things, as well as every article of European dress, from Madras, brought on the backs of Oxen which are the chief carriage of the country. By observing the latitude you will determine on what we are likely to meet with, as under the same climate, with cultivation, the same productions are commonly produced. Geography is a study that gives you a knowledge of every part of the known world without suffering cold, heats, from bad or no water and such provisions as can be got, and (what is very bad) shipwreck. I think we shall have a very great happiness in talking over many of the places I have visited, and how charmed shall I be to find my Jane knows more of many of them than I who have seen them. As I shall never be so happy as with my family I hope, when I come home, to be as little as possible out of your society. This whole world, my Jane, does not contain a person I love so much as your dear Mama. It is only because I had public duties to fulfil, and to encrease our very small fortune, that I could be prevailed upon to leave her for a day. One of the first things that made me so love your Mama was seeing her so dutiful, and good, and affectionate to her Mama.

I fear you do not remember our visits to Portsmouth and Wycombe, and Redbridge, and Aylesbury, you were then very little, but a great favorite with your papa. My dear Charles! you must write to, to tell him you have heard from me and that I shall feel a happiness I cannot express to see him a fine good boy, and fond of his Greek and Latin. My dear Jemima too! that I have never seen, I long to know.

I have made a long march to-day. The weather is very hot and I ought to beg you to excuse me for writing you such a hasty letter; for you know it is slovenly and often want of respect not to write as well as we can to every body. Do tell our dear Aunty Croke how much I long to see her. I am, my very dear Jane, with every warm affection of a father,

Yours
W. Harness

The " naughty Marattas " consisted of five federated states. The ruler of one of them, the Peshwa of Poona—the recognized head of the confederacy—had, as we have seen, come to terms with the British; but the other states, under two pre-eminent leaders, Sindhia of Gwalior and Holkar of Indore, were to prove a thorn in the side of Lord Wellesley. Two others, the Gaekwar of Baroda and the Bhonsla Raja of Nagpur, were also to cause trouble. The Mahratta warriors had been drilled by French officers and their armies were now formed on the European model—though whether in this form these swarms of essentially guerilla soldiers made a more efficient fighting force is perhaps doubtful. The Governor-General had a lively consciousness of a possible threat from France. Always in his mind was the thought of an invasion of India led by Bonaparte himself. This apprehension shaped his policy, for to him the power of the Mahrattas in India meant the future power of France.

The long and wearing, but highly successful march to Poona continued.

Camp, 28 March 1803

The heat is very great the thermometer 105 in tents and yesterday we did not get under cover till three in the afternoon. However with my horses, with excellent nourishment and good covering and rest I am able to undergo everything. They talk of a French war, I do think rather than let any thing detain me from you I would sell out, high as I am getting in my profession and, in this hour of exultation, I will say not without some little share of professional credit. Poona I understand is not more than 90 miles from Bombay; as soon as all is adjusted I will endeavor to get my Baggage from Madras, and embark from thence.

The 34-year-old general was clearly the man to conduct this march and the subsequent campaign. His experience of administration as Governor of Seringapatam and the intimate knowledge of the Mahratta people gained during his energetic pursuit of the brigand, Doondia; his natural shrewdness and courage and the penetrating understanding of the oriental mind that he had acquired—all these qualities were to stand him— and the army—in good stead.

At the end of April, after " almost crossing the peninsula ", the army was at last in camp near Poona. The Peshwa was back on his throne and Sindhia and Holkar had withdrawn in a threatening manner to the north.

Camp near Poona, May 1803

General Wellesley having had intimation of an intention to set fire to the Town, moved off with the Cavalry on the 19th and came here after a forced march of 56 miles on the 20th, having a very difficult Ghaut to descend on his route that detained him several hours; he was just in time to save the Capital from conflagration. I brought up the line and Pack on the 22nd, having marched in the last seven days 95 miles without a blade of forage for our cattle. The enemy constantly moved away on our approach, the Peishwar is very quietly in his capital. It is probable we shall not be able to leave the territory of the Marattah states till after the monsoon, as, with interests so discordant and with Chiefs so powerful, it is not to be expected they can quietly look on to the dismemberment of their empire, unawed by force. Our March has been long and toilsome; we are more, by the route it was necessary to take, than 900 miles from Madras. I never once got into my palanquin although the weather has been almost insufferably hot and we frequently did not arrive at the ground of encampment till four in the afternoon. Moving to the different parts of the line as my duty called me, there were few days I did not tire two horses. I had not an hour's sickness.

I have been obliged to buy Camels at a heavy expence and Bullocks and horses; corn now costs me 17 Rupees a day—and Servants' wages fifty pounds a month. I have been obliged to raise the wages of several who could not buy rice at the rate it is now sold. This command is certainly very honorable and flattering to me, but it will raise my reputation without my purse.

He was anxious now to get back to Madras for an October ship. " Should this country be settled I will make a run for it." In spite of the " insufferably hot weather ", " there never perhaps was an army more healthy than this " and, he noted with satisfaction, " never was there one from which dissipation was so completely excluded ".

The Peshwa, living quietly in his capital, evidently emerged on occasions. On 6 May Colonel Harness received amusing instructions to prepare as impressively as possible for a visit from this oriental ruler.

Dear Sir,

Major General Wellesley desires me to request that you will give orders for the Troops to be in readiness to fall in—at a moment's warning—and a Salute of 19 Guns, to be fired, as the Peishwah passes the Line to-morrow.

In order that the Corps of Infy may appear the stronger, the General also requests that you will order the Old Picquets to join their corps at sunrise—and the mounting of the new picquets to be deferred till the above Ceremony be over.

The Cavalry are to be ready as well as the Infy. Colonel Chase cannot even guess the probable time when *His Highness* will be pleased to pass the Line, otherwise it would be mentioned to you.

> I remain Dr Sir,
> Yrs obediently,
> R. Barclay

Tallegaum 6th May 1803

Any hopes of an immediate peaceful settlement proved illusive. In August the army had moved further northward and Wellesley fought a fierce and decisive battle at the taking of the important town of Ahmadnagar.

> Camp near Amednuger, 22 August 1803

Having placed the Paishwa on the Musnad and restored the country to tranquillity, we hoped to see the end of our labors. However Scindia and Bonnesla kept up their united armies in the borders of our ally the Nyzam. General Wellesley moved towards them and represented the impossibility of his quitting the Marattah territory so long as their force was held together on the Nyzam's frontier. They agreed to the treaties we had entered into with the Paishwa; they had not a grievance to represent from the British Government, but still parties of their predatory horse were even suffered to plunder countries belonging to our Ally. General Wellesley wrote in consequence to Colonel Collings our resident to leave Scindia's camp and to assure him he should look upon his holding his present hostile position as a sufficient reason for him to consider him as an enemy, and that he should act accordingly. He persisted, and Colonel Collings left him on the 2nd.

What renders his conduct most extraordinary is he has not one shilling in his Camp and his Troops are daily deserting from him for want of pay. The General, on receiving the news on the 7th of Colonel Colling's departure, marched on the 8th and captured the city of Amednugger, the richest Town in this part of Scindia's dominions, and having prepared everything for a seige on the 12th he took the Fort, considered almost impregnable. The General in his orders says his thanks are particularly due to Lieut Colonels Harness, Wallace and Max-

well commanding Brigades. The whole Country to the
Gadavry was instantly settled, a Collector appointed and native
troops raised to assist the revenue Officers. Colonel Collings
remains at Arungabad in daily expectation of receiving over-
tures from Scindia. Amednugger was the residence of the
famous Aurungzepe.[1] Affairs are considered as so near drawing
to a conclusion that General Stuart's army have returned to
quarters.

I was greatly in hopes that before this I should have been
enabled to fix the date of my leaving India, but this foolish
protracting infatuated people have drawn out their wretched
operations to a length unforeseen. Never was a Country pro-
ducing the finest crops, almost without cultivation, so wretched,
so distracted.

23 August

The Army is crossing the Godavery at Tokay about 30 miles
from Arungabad. You will see it in the Maps. Meybell's Map
of the Peninsula with his explanatory Book is the best you can
have to give the children a general knowledge of the geography
of the East.

Arungabad, 30 August

I have detained my letter day after day hoping to hear an
adjustment had been made but to no purpose. Scindia has
scattered his army into small bodies and is plundering the
Nizam's dominions; a war on the peasantry is cruelty, cowar-
dice and barbarity.

Colonel Harness's modest account gives little idea of the
gallant and dangerous part he played in the attack on Ahmadnagar. The town, which was quite distinct from the fort, was
surrounded by a high wall or *pettah*. We must go to Fortescue's
History of the British Army to fill in William Harness's story.

The right column was composed of the flank companies of
the Seventy-fourth and a battalion of Sepoys under Captain

---

[1] Aurangzeb, the great Mogul Emperor who lived from 1618 to 1707. A cruel
and ruthless monarch, he was yet regarded by the Mussulmans of India as one of
their greatest rulers. There are various spellings of his name.

Vesey, and the centre column of the battalion-companies of the Seventy-fourth and another battalion of Sepoys under Lieutenant-Colonel Wallace. The left column, commanded by Colonel Harness, reached the walls first, planted its ladders, and strove with the utmost gallantry to force its way into the town; but the men were hurled down as fast as they ascended, and after ten minutes abandoned the attempt, the seventy-eighth having lost six officers killed and some fifty men killed and wounded.[1]

An indication of the still disturbed state of the country is an order sent to Colonel Harness on 15 September—an order that he must have carried out with little relish.

Sir,

The Honble Major General Wellesley requests that you will order Major Dallas to march immediately with such part of his Battalion as is off duty, and with his Guns and one Tumbril, to the village of Terwarah, said to be three Coss [2] from Camp— and near to which the Bazar people were plundered yesterday, by a number of men on foot.

Direct Major Dallas to seize upon the Headman and ten or twelve of the other principal men of the place and bring them Prisoners to Camp. If resistance be made let him use the force at his command—and when he has secured the people let him make known to the Inhabitants that he carries them off to answer for the plunder of the Camp bazar men near that village.

Triparam, a man of the party plundered, will conduct the Battalion.

Capt. Mackay has been [desired] to send Gun bullocks.

R. Barclay
Dy Adj Gen.

Camp 15th Sept. 1803

Again the army moved northwards; the fiercest and most decisive battle of the whole Indian campaign was fought on 23 September at Assaye in Hyderabad. In this engagement William Harness again bore a prominent part.

[1] *A History of the British Army*, Vol. 5, Bk. XIII, p. 16—1910 edition.
[2] *Coss*—a measure varying in different parts of India from $2\frac{1}{2}$ to $1\frac{1}{4}$ miles.

Camp Essaie, 1 October 1803

A guardian Providence which has protected me through so many difficulties has preserved me unhurt in the battle from whence I date this letter. On the 23rd September as soon as we had arrived at the purposed ground of encampment Genl Wellesley learnt that the enemy was within five miles; he immediately determined to attack him. The Battle was very severe; my Brigade composed the first line, Colonel Wallace's the second line and our cavalry were in the rear. We had but six Battalions, the enemy had seventeen with Cavalry covering the whole country. The victory was complete. We took ninety-eight pieces of cannons and slept on the field of battle. We had marched twenty-four miles, our loss has been considerable. General Wellesley had his horse shot under him as had Colonel Wallace and myself. This will I trust close the war, as Scindia having lost his field train, this will prevent him from again facing us. Genl Wellesley's orders are very flattering to Wallace and me. This is said to be the most brilliant action that ever happened in India. With what real delight shall I receive my Bessy's congratulations on it.

27 November 1803

The General told me yesterday in confidence that he had concluded a suspension of hostilities with Scindiah; and the Rajah of Berar who is now the only man that holds out has never been at war for twenty years, and is in all respects unable to stand against the united forces. I have the most confident hope that peace will be restored in a very little month. Lord Wellesley in his letter of thanks after our battle looks upon the business as concluded. I fancy a division of captured property will very soon take place. I am led to understand my share in money, but chiefly in Jewels, will exceed a thousand pounds. We are now in the province of Eliehpoor about an hundred miles from Nagpur the capital of Berar. I have a horror of the miseries this infatuated man is drawing on his beautiful and rich country.

You will see General Wellesley's letter and the Governor-General's orders in the public prints, but as I hope this will get home before them, I will copy the paragraph in which I am named.

" His Excellency in Council directs Major General Wellesley to signify to the Officers and Troops employed on this glorious occasion, and especially to Lt Col. Harness and Lt Col. Wallace who commanded Brigades, and to the Officers of the Staff, the high sense entertained by the Governor-General in Council of their eminent and honorable services."

How Elizabeth's heart must have burned with pride on reading of the " eminent and honorable services " of the husband who, she confidently expected, would follow hard upon the heels of his letter. Yet it was only two days after he wrote that General Wellesley fought and won another battle at Argaon; and Colonel Harness was not there to take part in the victory. His health, which, so he constantly assured his Bessy, had been almost consistently good, broke down at last, and we know from General Wellesley's own account that he was so ill that the General was obliged to order him off the field. He wrote to his wife from hospital at Eliehpoor on 20 December:

My ever tenderly dear Bessy,

My letter of the 27th ulto. told you I was in the highest health. How surprized will you be to read in the General letter of 29th that I was absent from severe indisposition. On the 28th I felt unwell and drank plentifully of rice water; however I found myself not getting better and was attacked with fever. I came in here, the Doctors have filled me with mercury, my fever has left me and my appetite is become enormous. I have now no disease and am recovering my strength very fast. All accounts in camp speak of a very speedy peace. Ambassadors are in Camp to treat and it is impossible in my opinion it can be delayed beyond the end of the month. My adored Bessy I will fly to you. Nothing shall keep me one day in India after the peace. You know I have my leave in my pocket.

How very glorious has been this campaigne in all its parts and how necessary to check the french interest which had become uncommonly great. The Marattas are rendered peaceable for a lengthy period and the Brittish interests secured. It has detained me a year but it has given me some credit; it is the last I will pass from you.

185

He was better, and happy at the now almost certain prospect of an early return home; happy too in the " glorious campaigne " and his own honourable part in it. More than a year earlier he had written warning Elizabeth of the changes she might expect to see in him after so long a separation.

8 September 1802

You will expect to see me much changed; seven years will have wrought on a person that has always appeared advanced beyond my time of life. However I am not much more grey, and have not lost a tooth since I saw you. My Bessy will love her old husband.

In another letter he spoke of himself as " an old man that a variety of climates has assisted time in advancing the age of ".

It was not to be. Elizabeth was not to welcome back her " old husband " (he was about 42). The letter from Eliehpoor Hospital, so full of anticipation and of hopes of returning health, was his last; for he died a few days later on 2 January 1804. There is nothing to tell us what caused the fatal turn of his illness. His best friends were unable to be with him at the last; but one who saw him six days before he died records that " he was calm and collected, and appeared to await his Destiny with firmness and with resignation ". We may feel with certainty that this good, faithful soldier—" trusty and well beloved ", in the words of the King's commission—who had come unhurt through so much hard service and gallant action, met his lonely death with that " beautiful propriety " of which he had written long ago in Guernsey; and that assuredly when, without joy of comradeship or glory of battle, he passed over, " all the trumpets sounded for him on the other side ".

" His country has lost a brave and distinguished officer ", wrote his surgeon friend, Thomas Christie; " society a most valuable member, those who enjoyed his intimacy a most estimable friend." And Captain James Walch, the father of Charles's friend, wrote: " Every officer and soldier in the 80th Regt feels the death of that worthy Colonel with the utmost regret."

General Wellesley himself wrote, some months later, an

account of the Colonel's sickness and death. The letter was
addressed to Captain Harvey of the 80th Regiment, that same
young Harvey, we may suppose, who had been William
Harness's not always satisfactory protégé.

Camp at Eliehpour, 10 June 1804

Dear Sir,
    I received only last night your letter of the 25 April and I
beg to assure you that the respect and regard which you
profess for your late friend Colonel Harness have tended to
increase the good opinion which I had already entertained of
your character. . . .
    Colonel Harness was taken ill a day or two before the battle
of Argaum on the 29th Nov^{br}., and he was so unwell upon
that occasion as to be delirious when the Troops were going
into the action and I was obliged to order him into his Palanquin. After the battle of Argaum the Army made some rapid
marches towards Eliehpour in order to prevent the Enemy
from taking a new position under the protection of the fort of
Ganilghan which did Co. Harness no good; and on our arrival
at Eliehpour he went into that place for the benefit of his
health. He remained there during the siege of Ganilghan and
I saw him afterwards as the Army was marching through
Eliehpour towards Nagpour and he was much recovered.
Peace having been concluded with the Rajah of Berar, the
Army returned to the westward through Eliehpour; and I saw
Colonel Harness again much recovered; but he appeared to
have a shortness of breath which I attributed to weakness,
particularly as he had no complaint at that time, yet said that
he did not feel himself sufficiently recovered to join the Army,
a measure to which I earnestly urged him. The last time I
saw him was about the 25th Dec^{br}. and a few days afterwards
I heard of his Death . . .
Believe me, dear Sir,
Ever your most faithfully,
Arthur Wellesley

11

Charles and his Sisters

IT WAS several months before the dire news reached England. On 26 June 1804 John Harness, the naval surgeon, was still writing to his sister-in-law of " the pleasing prospect of soon seeing my dear Brother ". " How happy shall I be ", he says, " to congratulate him on his arrival!" The children were still joyfully expecting their father's return when one of them wrote in an old note-book, " Zamor has just called us all [to] Tea at six the 20th of May 1804 ". When the news of the Colonel's death at last reached Dronfield it was a different small boy from the child of three years ago who wrote to his mother. Already, it seems, Charles was bravely shouldering his responsibility as the only man of the family—a characteristic that constantly appeared in his letters as he grew older.

Brampton, 21 September 1804

My very dear Mama,

You cannot think how glad I am to hear that you are pretty well in health; as you say, What a change it is! But you may depend upon it, that I will make you as happy as I possibly can, by attending to my lessons when at school, and by being dutiful to you when at home. I feel very dull at times when I think about it, but when I do, I recollect that my dear Papa is in a much happier world than we are, and that we shall soon meet again.

Elizabeth now had to make a difficult decision. Lord Harrington, who was her boy's godfather, suggested that he should arrange for Charles to be admitted to the Royal Military College at Great Marlow, an institution of which he was a governor and where his own son was a pupil. The unhappy mother was fully alive to Lord Harrington's sympathetic

188

Charles Harness as a young man.

Mrs. Elizabeth Harness in later life.

anxiety to help her and to the advantages of the offer; but was Charles to be a soldier too?

You will not be surprised [she wrote to one of her aunts] that Lord Harrington's kindness in respect to my dear Boy was a shock to me. My first wish in regard to him was that I might be able to continue him with Mr Heyrick, and you will suppose I wished the Army might not be his choice; consequently that I hesitate to accept an offer that would at once decide his future situation in life. I was truly distressed and knew not what answer to make. I reflected that should the Army at a future period be the dear Boy's choice, that I should never forgive myself for having deprived him of that mode of Education so desirable for the profession. When he was last at home we perceived a strong inclination in him for the Army.

Soon, however, Elizabeth was reassured on some points. She was told that at Marlow the studies were " not confined to military knowledge ", that " education is there carried on upon that liberal basis that the young Gentlemen become qualified for other modes of life and may relinquish the Military profession "; and, most important of all to a fond parent, she heard from another mother that she was " delighted with [her son's] situation and perfectly satisfied with the institution and the conductors of the Seminary ". Mr Heyrick wrote that " he is qualified for any Examination, which Boys of his age may fairly be expected to undergo: and that as to his temper and behaviour, the Governors of the Institution at Marlow may expect to find in him a Pupil of good abilities, steady conduct, obliging manners, and tractable disposition ". The die therefore was cast, and at the age of 14 or so Charles became a gentleman cadet at Great Marlow.

The Royal Military College, the forerunner of Sandhurst, was opened in 1802 for a hundred gentleman cadets. Thirty of them were, like Charles, the sons of officers who had died on active service and were entitled to free education, board, and clothing. Twenty sons of serving officers were admitted for a fee of £40, and the sons of civilians paid £90 a year. The institution appears to have been strictly and wisely carried on. " Any Cadet ", ran the regulations, " who joins his Company

with a greater Sum of Money than ONE GUINEA, OR HAS ANY
SENT TO HIM FROM ONE VACATION TO ANOTHER, will subject
himself to be sent away from the College ". The weekly
allowance of pocket money was 2s., and no cadet was allowed
to contract any debts. Here is the young cadet's clothing list:

    8 shirts with Frills
    7 Pair of short Worsted Stockings
    7 Pair of Cotton Ditto
    8 Pocket Handkerchiefs
    6 Towels
    4 Night-caps
    4 Pair of Stocking Web Drawers
    2 Pair of strong Shoes
    1 Bible
    1 Prayer Book
    1 small Looking-glass
    1 Clothes Brush, and Tooth Brushes
    1 large, and 1 small Tooth Comb
    1 small foul Clothes Bag made of Ticken

By the time that Charles went to Marlow the family had left
Derbyshire and were living near Elizabeth's relations at
Aylesbury. In 1809 they moved to Stanmore in Middlesex.
The boy's letters show him capable, upright, amusing, affectionate, full of loving concern for his widowed mother and his
two young sisters. His dry college reports indicate that his
marks were good, though the non-committal statement, " Progress equal to the time employed ", is as far as the authorities
allowed themselves to go in the matter of praise. There is
suggestion of an outbreak of high spirits in a bill that his
mother had to pay for " damage to Fortification instruments "
and another of a shilling only for " share of fire irons and
drawer handles and locks destroy'd dormitories ". In the
gentleman cadet's letters to his sisters—loving, teasing, saucy
letters—he complains sometimes of the infrequency of their
correspondence. " Don't faint or rave at the beginning of this
letter ", he writes as the heading of a missive to the errant
Jane; and continues:

My dearest Jane,

Why have I not heard from you? I have even thought that you were offended at my saying that I would not write to you *out of spite* [because she had not written to him]. But, however, be that as it may; if you do not forgive me, I forgive you.

In 1807 Charles passed " a very strict examination before the Duke of Kent " and brought back " a Certificate to shew that I am fit to serve in His Majesty's Army ". In August of the following year the cadets were reviewed by the Prince of Wales.

He said [wrote Charles to his mother], that upon his honor, he was never so much delighted in his life, that no regiment could have done better; and though I say it that should not say it, He asked who I was, and said I was a very fine young fellow; the Duke of Clarence was with him, and said the same. There was likewise a very fine show of female beauties in the College Grounds; I only wished for *you* to make it *compleat*. All the neighbourhood were here to see *the King that is to be*, as I heard some of the Lower Class say. We had a suspension of Studies on the 12th [his birthday]. I drank some Wine with some other Cadets, one of the Toasts was " The Prince of Wales, Long may he continue so ". Don't you think it a very good one?

Elizabeth's foreboding was justified, and Charles would be a soldier. In 1809 he sailed with his regiment—the 80th, it goes without saying—for India. He was not yet 17. His miniature, as he must have looked about this time, shows an attractive curly-haired young man in blue coat and ample white stock with a good open face and steady brown eyes. His farewell letter to his sisters shows, as did his father's letters, something of the trials of separation in those days of slow journeys and uncertain posts. It is a mixture of courageous facing of the parting, some characteristic teasing, and an expression of elder-brotherly concern for the girls' ladylike conduct. His mother was evidently with him in the Isle of Wight. Jemima apparently was at school, but not, we may be sure, at one of those " affected schools " such as her father would have disapproved.

191

Newport, Isle of Wight, 9 February 1809

My dear Jane and Jemima,

I have this day received orders to hold myself in readiness to embark for India on Saturday, on board the Perseverance.

I was in hopes of having seen you, my dear Sisters, in the Isle of Wight but it cannot be helped now, and it is what must be expected in a Soldier's life. Mama has written to Mrs Davies to tell her that dear Jemima will not go back before the end of the first quarter, which I dare say will not be unfavourable tidings. We have got very comfortable lodgings, and they would have been much more so, could you have been with us.

There is a very nice and elegant young man in the 80th at this Depôt of the name of Brown, who would make a very nice husband for my dear Jane, and a little fellow about a head and a half shorter than I am that would make another for Jemima. So you see I am looking out for you already. Depend upon it that I shall write every opportunity that offers, and do pray do the same, as it will be a source of comfort to me.

Perhaps you, my dearest girls, may not have an opportunity of hearing from me again for these six months, but depend upon it, you will never be from my thoughts. Pray, dear Jemima, practise regularly at Miss Woodcock's. I shall have an opportunity of learning the flute on the voyage. Do not read any more novels, but read clever books to my aunt. Adieu, once more, my dearest Sisters. Adieu.

Colonel and Mrs Norris were back in the East, and proved kind hosts to the son of their old friend. A letter from the Colonel gives a glimpse of Charles on his arrival at Madras.

2 September 1809

My dear Madam,

We were made very happy by the receipt of your kind letter by your dear Son, who is indeed a very fine young Man. He had been a month in the country before he found us out and only a few days before he was ordered to join his corps at Bangalore, which is about 200 miles from this. But during those few days we had the pleasure of his company, I believe, some part of every day; poor fellow, he struck me as being very like my dear friend, his Father. He is indeed a very fine Youth and it really grieved us to think what you must have felt at parting with him.

The young man introduced himself to me and said his name was Harness; judge of my astonishment for I had not the least idea of ever seeing the Son of my much lamented friend in India. Be assured, my dear Madam, he will ever be most heartily welcomed by Mrs Norris and myself, who was equally surprised with me when I introduced him to her as the son of our darling Seringa's God-Papa.

He left Madras in high health and spirits, and I have no doubt he will do very well particularly as the climate does not seem to disagree with him; and from what we saw of his disposition I am sure he will always find friends. He seems a modest, well-bred, Gentlemanlike youth and must ever be a comfort to you.

Charles gave his own version of the visit.

22 September 1809

My best compliments to Major Harvey, and tell him how grateful I am to him for his kindness and the introductory letters which made me very comfortable at Madras. Col. and Mrs Norris are particularly kind, they are at Madras talking of going home. They tell me I must look upon them as my Father and Mother; they are rather methodistical, quite plain people.

Another old friend of Charles's father, Dr Christie, had sent him a letter, " very kind and full of good advice ". In this same letter of 22 September we learn that the prize money, for which William Harness had sacrificed so much, had at last been paid. " I sincerely congratulate you, my dear Mama, upon at last obtaining the Seringapatem prize money, which Christie tells me is 2600£." (It appears that five years later a second instalment was paid.)

Two days later this devoted brother wrote to 13-year-old Jemima:

I do not know what I shall find to bring home for you, there are plenty of beautiful Parrots and Monkeys. Would you like ivory fans or anything of that kind. I think I will bring you a *wild Tyger*, or a *Rattlesnake*, or perhaps an *Alligator* as I dare say you would be fond of such Company.

In another letter he remembers a small cousin:

Tell little Henry [1] that I will bring him a big Bow and Arrow, such as the Black fellows fight with, but he must promise not to hurt anyone with it.

These light-hearted suggestions were rather premature, for Charles was to stay nearly six years in India. Writing to Jane in February 1812 he broke the news that, though it was now three years since they parted, he feared that " that time would again elapse before we meet ".

During those six years Charles wrote home cheerfully and constantly, and his letters are full of news. He dances, he has " again taken to the Flute ", he " keeps a very nice horse ", he acts, he is captivated by various young ladies, he gets into debt—a Lieutenant's pay was very small—he proves himself a keen and useful member of his profession. He writes to his sisters of " a pleasant hunting excursion with Colonel Forbes ".

13 October 1811

The Rajah of Coorg [2] amused me much, he was dressed in a Field Marshall's uniform, with a *common* Star on his breast. Colonel Forbes told him that it was not sufficiently handsome, and that our King wore a diamond one, upon which he immediately gave orders for one to be ready in three days. His Subjects hold him in great Awe, and in addressing him call him *Sawmy*, which signifies God, and prostrate themselves on the ground. He entertained us magnificently, elegant dinner, and every kind of wine. He gave me a knife *with a golden hilt*, it is shaped something like a Bill Hook, and is the common weapon of the country. He likewise gave me a Sandal Wood walking stick. He was rather indisposed himself, therefore could not accompany us out hunting, but gave orders that

[1] Afterwards General Sir Henry Harness, K.C.B.

[2] Probably the State of Coorg.

every thing should be prepared for us, about 18 miles from his Capital, which was the best part of the country for good sport. When we arrived there (in the midst of the jungle) although the order had been given only about 8 hours, a complete village seemed to have been raised by Enchantment. We had Elephants, Horses, Palankeens, or any conveyance we wished.

Brown is now on leave in Bengal, gone with his mother and lovely Sister to see his Brother in Law and eldest sister. You must not quiz me about Eliza Brown. She is the sweetest girl I have ever seen, and I am much quizzed by the Officers about her. Marriage is out of the question, as I can hardly keep myself, and she has not a farthing.

At another hunting-party, given by the same Rajah who was " remarkably civil to Europeans ", he was " much diverted ".

We killed two Royal Tygers, one an immense one, besides *Sambors* (a very large species of Deer) and wild Buffaloes. We rode out on Elephants, and when we arrived at the Hunting Ground were perched up in trees, with plenty of ammunition, while about a thousand of the Rajah's people, with noise of Drums, Horns and their own *screaching* drove the animals towards us from the midst of the jungle.

He sent Jane a description of the coming-of-age of another Indian prince.

Seringapatam, 2 February 1812

The day before yesterday the Hon^rble Mr Cole, British resident at Mysore gave a splendid party to our regiment. The occasion was the ceremony of the Rajah's taking upon himself the administration of the affairs of his Kingdom, after his minority. We all attended the *Durbar* (or Court), where after seeing some Royal Tygers, and the wild animals let loose in a square surrounded by net work, Mr Cole presented the Rajah from the East India Company with five lacks of rupees, an elephant with a magnificent Houdah of Silver, two Beautiful Arabian Horses, a pair of shawls, some elegant Necklaces of Diamonds, with bunches of Precious stones pendent from them, an ornament of Jewels for the Turban, and a beautiful sprig for the head, of Diamonds, and an elegant Sword mounted in Gold. Although in general the Rajah makes presents of Shawls to Gentlemen and Ladies who attend Durbar, yet the shabby fellow did not make any in return for the magnificent ones His Black Majesty got himself. After this we had an elegant dinner and dance at the Residency. Mr Cole is one of the finest fellows I ever met, of very free and engaging manners and a perfect gentleman. Few *Ladies* have seen him without being *captivated*.

The young soldier was keenly interested in all the little doings at home and in details of the new home at Stanmore. A fellow officer had told him that it was " the most pleasant place he was ever at ", the people " all very genteel and respectable " and " remarkably good to the poor ". He was sometimes homesick, but usually he enjoyed his varied and interesting life. On 9 October he wrote from Seringapatam, " I have received on my dear Father's account a very handsome medal on account of the capture of this place. My dearest Mama may well conceive that I am not â little proud of it."

Seringapatam, 11 October 1812

My dearest Jane,

Would to God I were with you, and accompanying you at all your Balls and in all your rides. In India we are completely exiles. We have had but one dance at Seringapatam since our arrival. That was certainly a pleasant one. You must know, dear Jane, that I am a great *Lady's Man*, and *shall certainly*, unless you guard them against it, *captivate the hearts* of *all* the young ladies at Stanmore. Do you think that you can find one of sense and beauty that will ensnare mine in return ?

And eighteen months later:

Quilon, 16 April 1814

My own dearest Sisters,

We make as much of Quilon as is possible and I assure you have a great deal of gaiety, and the 80th itself contribute largely to it. We have built a very pretty little Theatre. I appeared for the first time in the character of *Captain Absolute* in the *Rivals*, and, though I say it who should not say it, gained a great deal of applause. James, Mrs Shaw and myself all drank dear Jemima's health in a bumper on the 31st March, and we shall not forget dear Jane's on the 15th of July.

We hear too that James Walch played the part of Mrs Malaprop " most admirably ". Charles records with some satisfaction that he has now attained the height of five feet eight (the Harnesses were not a tall race),

Where I suppose I shall stop. I was quite astonished to hear of Dear Jemima being the tallest of you, as dear Jane was taller than I was on leaving England. However you are both a most captivating height, which I dare say many a swain can attest.

In 1813, following the then existent practice, Mrs Harness bought her son a captaincy.

Seringapatam, 28 February 1813

How can I sufficiently thank you, my dearest Mama, for the purchase of my company? I have seen my promotion in the Gazette, and my name as a Captain in the Army list.

All through that year Charles was eagerly hoping for leave and in December we find him drawing out money for the expenses of the voyage to England. But it was not until 1815 that the prospect of leave became almost a certainty. In preparation for his home-coming he wrote a frank, penitent letter about his money difficulties.

Quilon, 3 January 1815

My ever dearest Mother,

My application for leave of absence has been forwarded by the Commander-in-Chief at Madras to Lord Moira for his approval, so that I have now little doubt of success. I am therefore making every arrangement, and I trust before the middle of next month that I shall be on my voyage to Old England, to the best of mothers and to my dearest Sisters. I cannot keep from myself, my dearest Mama, that I am returning to you as the Prodigal Son, for I have been shamefully extravagant. I shall have much of this nature to confess to you, and I rely on your goodness, which you have ever shown me, to grant me your forgiveness. But this let me assure you of, Heaven knows it is the only Vice I have been guilty of. I never was a Gambler. I have never ventured nor ever lost or won to the value of a Pagoda. I have never been addicted to drinking. I can write in this manner to a Mother without being accused of self commendation, but true as what I have said it, nothing can atone for my extravagance.

Three days later Charles wrote again on a very different subject. There had been frequent mention in his correspondence of Mrs Shaw, a young widowed sister of his friend, James Walch, who " is to me a brother ". Probably Mrs Harness was not taken entirely by surprise when her son, in a rapturous letter, announced his betrothal—subject to his mother's consent—to the lady of whom he had written three years before:

Mrs Shaw has been some time a widow, and is now but 22. She was married when only 14; what a pity that she should have been thus thrown away on such a brute as her husband is represented as having been! She is a most pleasing woman of extremely genteel manners and very well informed, for which she deserves the whole credit of instructing herself.

Mrs Shaw and her sister were returning to England and Charles looked forward to being home in July and introducing his Katherine to his relations. " You must and will admire her, and be equally proud of her with myself."

It was Charles's last letter from India. There was a note written on the voyage full of happy anticipation; and now tragedy, swift and crushing, once more visited this family. In May 1815 the charming and well-loved young soldier was drowned on his way home to England. The transport *Arniston* was wrecked off Cape Lagullas with only six survivors; and Charles was buried in a nameless grave on the coast of South Africa. He was 23 years old.

There is no record to show how the women of the family faced their new bereavement. " Oh surely I do possess something like fortitude ", Elizabeth had written once in a time of keen anxiety; and as surely we may feel that that fortitude did not desert her now. The final word is with James Walch, and contains a generous gesture from a faithful friend. Here is the document:

Quilon, 14 September 1815

I, Lieutenant James W. H. Walch, do hereby certify that I wave any claim I may be supposed to have to the late Captain Harness's Company (as Senior Lieutenant of the 80th Regiment) should His Royal Highness the Prince Regent be graciously pleased to allow of the said company being sold for the benefit of his Family.

J. Walch
Lt. 80th Reg^t

To end this chronicle in a happier vein, here are letters from Jane and Jemima which show the young ladies suitably engaged in pursuit of health and the accomplishments of gentility. Jane, according to her brother's surmise, had become " an excellent draftswoman " (she had sent him a drawing of the house at Stanmore), and Jemima " a great adept in music ".

" My dear Mama ", wrote Jane in a beautiful neat, sloping hand,

As Jemima has written so short a letter, I will endeavour to recollect something to add. I hear the East India Fleet is expected, so I hope we shall have a letter from dear Charles. This time next year we shall expect him and then as you say we may go into Buckinghamshire together. I think you will be pleased with my drawing. I have just finished a large group of flowers, you know you wished me to do them large. With Mr dr Fleury I am drawing Mount Vesuvius, it is to be varnished to look like oils. I think you will like it. Jemima goes on very well with her Music. I would add more but I am just going to take a walk with Mr Brown. I remain,

My dear Mama,
Your affectionate daughter
Jane Harness

Jemima wrote vivaciously from Brighton, where she had apparently been sent for the sake of her health.

16 October 1811

Mrs Bearcroft [her hostess] is an old woman of between fifty and sixty, very fat and dressed in black and french grey. She has three daughters, Miss Kitty (who lisps), Miss Fanny and Miss Sukey. I put on my dark gown this morning as I thought it would not be congruous to wear the light coloured gowns now and the Black Stuff one hereafter. I have a bed-room to myself and here I am sitting writing. I have been this morning to see the people bathe and I am sure I shall not like it at all, for they are carried out of the machine between two immense women, who dip them into the Sea, and when they come out all their clothes (to be sure they have nothing but a bathing gown) stick to them, while all the gentlemen stand and laugh at them. I am to go in to-morrow morning. Though last not least (for I am sure I have been thinking of you all along) I hope you got home safely last night and that you found Anne's cold almost well with Jane and Betsey's nursing; and I hope Eliza's is now really well. Pray give my love to them. Heigh-ho!

I wish I wish I wish in vain,
I wish I was at home again.

I wish you would send me some books, those travels in Sicily and Malta and those kind of books and my prayer book. Do not let me stay longer than a month. I wish too for a pair of new walking shoes, a brown silk cap and a bottle of ink, and do not let me go back in the coach, for it is so disagreeable I cannot bear it.

The miniatures of the sisters, painted to be sent to their brother in India, have not survived. It is reported that Jane was a beauty but, in spite of their brother's early efforts on their behalf, neither of these lively girls ever married. We hear of them in later middle age as two maiden ladies living together at Malvern. Of Elizabeth we have no further record except a strong, kindly face shown in a miniature painted in her later years. When Joseph Nollekens died in 1823 she had become the richer by several hundred pounds. The sculptor himself

left £300 to Mrs Harness of Stanmore " a cousin of my dear
late wife "; and Mrs Nollekens had left, to come to Elizabeth
after her husband's death, a share in some house property—
which was sold—situated in Bolsover Street and in Mortimer
Street, where the Nollekens had lived for many years.

Her daughter, Jemima, lived on well into the 1860s. My
mother had childish memories of a rather plain old lady who
was her cousin, Jemima Harness. She wore a white cap with
goffered frills all round her face and had a little pudding
specially made for her every day. She drank cocoa into which
she dipped her buttered toast, a proceeding which horrified
her small cousin; but of the " drollery " which, according to
her mother, was so marked a feature of " little Bessy's " early
years, there was no recollection. That is the last glimpse that
we have of this simple, honourable family, who, like many other
families in conditions not so far distant in time, and yet
so different from our own, lived and loved and sorrowed,
feared God, served their neighbours, and enjoyed life. And in
their letters they live still.

The Wreck of the Arniston

A narrative taken from the surviving crew relative to the loss of the Arniston *transport, wrecked near Cape Lagullas, on the evening of the 30th of May,* 1815:

Charles Stewart Scott, late carpenter's mate of the Arniston transport, and others, assert to the best of their knowledge, that she sailed from Point de Gall, on or about the 4th of April, under convoy of his Majesty's ship Africane, and Victor brig, with six Indiamen; about the 26th of May parted company from the convoy, owing to stress of weather, having blown away most of her sails, others were then bent; but the weather continued very squally with a heavy sea. On the 29th, about 7 a.m. the land was discovered right-a-head, bearing about N. by W. a long distance off, the wind then S.S.E.: about half-past 4 p.m. still blowing very strong, hauled to the wind on the larboard tack, under a close-reefed main-top-sail, and stood on till half-past 2 a.m. on the 30th; then supposing the land was near Table Bay, the hands were turned up, bore up, steering N.W. and set the foresail, intending to run for St Helena; continued on till 10 a.m. when the land was discovered nearly a-head; turned the hands up, and hauled the ship close to the wind on the larboard tack, still blowing very hard, made all sail, having topsails and courses set, stood on till near noon, when breakers were discovered on the lee bow, wore ship, and hauled to the wind on the other tack, stood on till 2 p.m. then wore and hauled to the wind on the larboard tack, continuing on till near 4 o'clock, when breakers were seen, which proved Lagullas Reef, which we could not weather on either tack, being completely embayed; clewed up the sails, and cut away three anchors; the two bower cables parted shortly after, when Lieutenant Brice, agent for transports, recommended the Captain to cut the sheet cable, and run the ship ashore, the only chance of saving the people's lives; the cable was then cut, and the ship put before the wind, and in about eight minutes after, she struck forward, the ship heeling to windward; cut away the guns in order to heel her the other way, which could not be effected, consequently she soon began to break up; about eight o'clock the masts went; and the ship, in a very short time was quite in pieces. Many people were drowned below, in consequence of her heeling to windward; and others clung to the wreck, endeavouring to reach the shore, about 1½ mile distant. Out of the whole crew, consisting of near 350 persons, only six men reached the shore, with great difficulty, upon planks, being much bruised by the surf and wreck, which was very high. At day-light the next morning the stern post was the only part of the ship to be seen; the beach was covered with wreck, stores, etc. and a number of dead bodies (which were buried by the survivors) and among whom were lord and lady Molesworth, the agent, and captain, with some children. On the next day, the first of June, considering ourselves to the westward of Cape Point, it was agreed to coast the beach to the eastward, which we continued to do for four days and a half, subsisting on shell-fish from off the rocks; but fearing we had taken a wrong direction, it was agreed to return to the wreck, and we accomplished it in three days and a half, where we remained six days, subsisting chiefly on a cask of oatmeal which had been driven on shore; by drying it in the sun we experienced great relief from it. The pinnace had been driven on shore bilged, which we proposed to repair in the best manner circumstances would allow; and endeavour to coast along the shore; at that time, the 14th of June, being at work on the boat, we were fortunately discovered by a farmer's son, John Swarts, who was out shooting, and humanely carried by him to his father's house, where we remained with every comfort he could afford us, for a week; and then set off for Cape Town, where we arrived on Monday evening the 26th of June.

Before we left the country we were informed that 331 bodies, thrown on shore, had been interred near the beach.

(Signed) C. STEWART SCOTT, and Party.

This declaration was made before me at Cape Town, the 27th day of June, 1815, of which this is a true copy.

(Signed) J. MERES,

Lieut. R.N. and A.T.

Zamor's Letter of Introduction

The following is a translation of the letter on page 77 above:

This letter will be delivered to you by one, Zamor, who is leaving for Portsmouth with the desire to do all that in him lies to give you satisfaction. By nature shy, he requires to be gently led. As for his loyalty, I am as ready to vouch for that as I am for my own, and I trust that, if ever I have the pleasure of making your acquaintance, you will have no cause to reproach me on that score. It is for this assurance that I am taking the liberty of recommending him to you, as a young person whom I have brought up from the age of nine years, and to whom I am greatly attached. But for the misfortunes which have torn my unhappy country, I should never have parted from him. Peace will shortly be made, and we shall be exiled from it for ever, and I shall myself be only too glad perhaps to be able to find a post rather more suited to my taste than is the occupation that I am now obliged to follow in order to provide daily bread for persons who have fallen upon adversity through no fault of their own. I do not even say that I may not later ask you to assist me by recommending me to your friends. Destined for service with the artillery, I am acquainted with mathematics and geography, as well as the science of fortification, and I would willingly undertake the education of one or two young people, to whom I could at the same time teach French. And here, Sir, I must beg your indulgence for having spoken to you of myself, when the only subject I was having to deal with was one entirely unconnected with myself: and I resume the original course of my letter in order to request that if, by circumstances unforeseen, you should be unable to retain Zamor as your servant, you would be so kind as to recommend him to your acquaintances in order to procure him a post. I will not speak to you of his wages: 30 guineas is rather a small amount for food, laundry and upkeep, but I have no doubt that when you find him attentive to your requirements you will give him sufficient to live on in reasonable comfort.

I have the honour to be, Sir, with deepest respect,

Your obedient servant

P. Regnier.

A Visit to Studley in 1716

Among the Harness letters is a copy of an account of a visit to Studley paid by one Herne in 1716. (Was this perhaps Thomas Hearne, the famous Oxford antiquary and Non-juror?)

March 31st Saturday

This morning a little before five o'Clock I walked over to Studely five miles from Oxford on purpose to see that place having never been there before. I was mightily pleased with the Manor House, tho' I was not in it, by reason I did not care to give any trouble to the inhabitants; but I was in the Chapel. Richard and Edward buried in the Chapel were brothers to James Croke Esqr now Lord of the Manor, who lives with his Sister Charlotte Croke, the said two here buried were the eldest and youngest brothers. The Father is also buried here, but nothing is yet put up to his memory. He died about two years since. This is a very small Chapel, they bury at Beckley. The Chapel adjoins to the Manor House. The greatest part of the Manor House of Studley is of a modern erection (being built by Judge Croke who also built the Almshouses) but the other parts are very ancient, particularly those at the East end, and the Kitchen too as they tell me, tho' I was not in the Kitchen; but I am told the present Mr Croke and his Sister too would have willingly shewed me the whole house if I had desired it, or let them but know of my being there. This Gentleman and his Sister are both young and live together, neither of them being married. Their Mother also lives with them mostly above stairs, being in a melancholy drooping condition occasioned as I am told, by her Husband Captain Croke who died about two years since, and used to go much astray. She has been a handsome woman and used formerly to be much at the old Earl of Abingdon's both at Rycant and

Wightham; it was at the Earl's house that the said Captain Croke courted her.

The Alms House at Studely is a pretty place enough. It is for four men and four women. They have 2s. a week each, and which is paid them constantly every Sunday in the Chapel at Studely, besides Gowns and firing and rooms and some other advantages, and one of them hath 20s. as an addition for reading of prayers every day morning and Evening.

INDEX

209